The Back Nine

E. A. Briginshaw

ISBN: 978-0-9921390-6-3 (Book)
ISBN: 978-0-9921390-7-0 (eBook)

ACKNOWLEDGMENTS

Although the novel is a work of fiction, some of the characters are composite characters based on my family and friends. Thanks to all of the people who reviewed and critiqued numerous drafts of this novel including friends, members of my family and writers from the London Writers Society.

This novel is dedicated to my mother, Frances Briginshaw, who is eighty-six years old as I write this. She roller-bladed until she was eighty, never wearing a helmet, claiming she'd just dive toward the grass alongside the path if she felt she was going to fall. She says it has been all downhill since eighty-two, but she continues to try every day, even on her "bad days". I am only about ten years into my experience of life after fifty, but I have seen through my mother's eyes what I can expect to encounter over the next twenty-five (hopefully more) years. She is my inspiration.

E. A. BRIGINSHAW

Table of Contents

Chapter 1: Wake-Up Call 1
Chapter 2: First Tee Jitters 9
Chapter 3: Staying on Plane 15
Chapter 4: Mid-Life Crisis 23
Chapter 5: One is A Lonely Number 29
Chapter 6: Nobody Said It Was Easy 36
Chapter 7: Father/Son Competition 42
Chapter 8: Taking Care of Mom & Dad..........................45
Chapter 9: Old Versus New...52
Chapter 10: Trying New Ways..61
Chapter 11: Changing Teams 70
Chapter 12: Getting Help..75
Chapter 13: Christmas Presents...82
Chapter 14: The Southern Swing.......................................91
Chapter 15: Amen Corner 99
Chapter 16: Tempo & Timing 113
Chapter 17: Money Games..121
Chapter 18: A Marathon, Not a Sprint 131
Chapter 19: League Play 139
Chapter 20: Black Friday 149
Chapter 21: The Rescue Club 159
Chapter 22: Foreplay..166
Chapter 23: Integrity Of The Game 172
Chapter 24: The S-Word 183
Chapter 25: Thunder & Lightning....................................193
Chapter 26: Toward The Light...203
Chapter 27: The Back Nine 215

E. A. BRIGINSHAW

CHAPTER 1: WAKE-UP CALL

It was an absolutely perfect autumn day when Jerry arrived at the golf course. The leaves on the hills overlooking the river valley in Southwestern Ontario were a brilliant mixture of reds, golds and yellows. It was cool, but not cold enough to trigger a frost delay to prevent the golfers from pursuing their favourite pastime.

Jerry was a starter at the golf course and once again, had been forced to get up at the crack of stupid to get there before the first golfers arrived. There was something magical about being one of the first golfers of the day to tee off and watch your ball land on freshly manicured fairways and greens, and there were always a few keeners trying to get out before the first "official" tee time.

Jerry was in his late sixties and had been semi-retired for several years. Although being a starter only paid minimum wage, Jerry loved the job. It required the people skills of a concierge at a five-star hotel along with the organizational skills of an air traffic controller. Just get people organized and off the first tee at their allotted time. Sounds simple enough. Most days it was relatively easy, but on others, it was like herding cats.

Jerry entered the back-shop area of the pro shop and found Murray pulling golf bags from the storage racks and moving them outside in preparation for the arrival of the golfers. As he pulled each bag, he put a tick-mark beside their name on the tee sheet.

"Bit cold for shorts, isn't it?" Jerry said.

"Not at all," Murray replied. Murray was also in his sixties and had worked at the golf course since it opened almost twenty years ago. He had originally been a member of the grounds crew, but decided about six years ago to take a "cushier" job in the back-shop.

Murray always wore shorts, whether it was the hottest day of the summer or threatening to snow in the last few days of the golf season. Although he wouldn't admit it, Murray was in competition with the other back-shop staff as to who could go the latest into the year wearing shorts. He always won.

"What cart do you want me to take for sand and seed?" Jerry asked.

"Take number fourteen. It gave us a problem yesterday and I don't want to send it out with any of the members until we're sure it's fixed."

Jerry started loading the bottles into the cart. The bottles consisted of a mixture of sand and grass seed that were used by the golfers to fill in their divots. A bottle was given to each golfer when they teed off, but the starter was responsible for placing extra bottles on the third and twelfth tees for those who forgot to pick one up before they teed off or ran out during their round.

"Be back shortly," Jerry said as he jumped into the cart.

"Don't forget your walkie-talkie," Murray yelled.

All staff were supposed to carry a two-way radio with them so they could be reached wherever they were on the course, but Jerry had always wondered whether it was worth it. Most days, he didn't use it at all. He trudged back into the pro shop and clipped one onto his belt.

Riverview wasn't just a golf course; it was a gated golf community with houses and condos overlooking the various holes. It was targeted at people over fifty who were retired, or near retirement, and who had led pretty successful lives. This was where they wanted to spend their golden years and the lifestyle wasn't cheap. As Jerry drove the cart through the community toward the twelfth tee, he waved at a few people who were tending their flower gardens or out for an early morning walk.

"Good morning, Jerry," one of the owners said when he went by.

"Good morning, Mr. Ferguson," Jerry said with a wave and a smile. Even though he knew the man's first name was Ray, the staff were instructed to always address the members formally by their last names.

When Jerry arrived at the twelfth tee, he loaded the new sand and seed bottles into the holder, picked up the empty ones, and placed them in his cart to take back to the pro shop. He waved to the guy cutting the twelfth green. The grounds crew had arrived at the course earlier than Jerry, many starting their day before the sun was even up.

As he took the shortcut along the trees toward the third tee, Jerry was impressed once again by the beauty of the property. In this part, the golf course dropped down toward the river valley and it bordered on environmentally protected areas that were home to numerous rare trees and flowers. There were trails through the woods that were used by members of the

3

Riverview community for early morning or late evening walks. That's when you were most likely to encounter deer or other protected wildlife.

As Jerry followed the path behind the second green, he caught a glimpse out of the corner of his eye of something red in the forest. *Probably just some leaves.* He'd check it out on his way back.

When he reached the third tee, he placed the new sand and seed bottles in the holder and picked up the empties. As he headed back, he slowed down looking for the red object in the forest, but nothing caught his eye. He got out of the golf cart and started walking back, veering onto a small path that led into the forest.

There it was. He was sure it was a red jacket. Someone probably dropped it when they were out for a walk. But as he approached, he had the strange feeling that something wasn't right. That's when he realized that it wasn't just a red jacket. Someone wearing a red jacket was lying on the ground, just off the edge of the trail. He raced forward and gently rolled the body over.

"Glen," he said, when he recognized who it was.

There was no response.

"Glen, are you alright?" he said as he tried to rouse him.

Again, there was no response. He could see a red welt on the side of Glen's face. He must have fallen and hit his head. He grabbed his wrist and felt for a pulse, but didn't feel anything. *Heart attack?* He started doing chest compressions, but then noticed that Glen wasn't breathing. *ABC - ABC. Airway, Breathing, Compression. Shit, I was supposed to check his breathing before doing chest compressions!* He quickly tilted Glen's head back and opened his mouth. *Why wasn't he breathing?*

Jerry could feel his own heart beating like it was about

4

to explode. *I need help!* He started to run back toward the golf cart, but stopped when he remembered that he had the walkie-talkie clipped to his belt.

"Help, Help. I need help!" he screamed into the two-way radio.

There was no response. He checked to make sure it was turned on. The green light showed that it was and it was set to channel two. *Why wasn't anyone answering?*

"Help. I need help right away!" he screamed into the walkie-talkie again.

When he didn't get a response, he decided to race over to get help from the guy cutting the twelfth green. He had only taken a few steps when he heard the crackle of the radio.

"Jerry, is that you?" Murray asked. "What's the problem?"

"Yeah, it's me. I need help. I found Glen on a trail behind the second green. He's unconscious."

It was only a few more seconds until he got another response, but it seemed like an hour.

"Scott just called 9-1-1. Help is on the way." There was a pause of a few seconds. "You said Glen is hurt. Glen, who?"

Even though Jerry knew Glen's last name, his head was spinning and he couldn't remember it. For some reason, Glen's bag number popped into his head. "276," he said.

Murray knew everyone's bag number. "Glen Watkins?"

"Yes," Jerry said. "I don't think he's breathing. I'm going to try mouth-to-mouth."

Jerry dropped to his knees and tried to revive him, but he could tell it wasn't working. It was only a few minutes later when the supervisor of the grounds crew arrived on a golf cart and took over. He had an emergency kit and a defibrillator with him and had been trained to deal with medical emergencies. But he had no luck reviving Glen either. The ambulance arrived less than five minutes later, but Jerry could see from the paramedics that there was nothing they could do.

Jerry felt like he was going to throw up. *Why didn't I stop the first time?* He'd never seen anyone die before. He never wanted to see it again.

* * *

The death of Glen Watkins shocked the entire community. Since Riverview was a senior's community, they were used to losing a few people every year. But those were people who were well into their eighties or nineties, or those who were known to be battling cancer.

It wasn't supposed to happen to guys like Glen. He was only fifty-two. He was in great shape. He played golf at least three times a week and always walked and carried his own golf bag. "Power carts are a waste of money," he always used to say.

In the winter months, he played hockey. And not in some huff-and-puff league; he played with guys in their twenties and thirties and took pride that he could outskate most of them.

The autopsy revealed that Glen had died of a brain aneurysm. There had been no warning. In fact, he'd had a complete physical about six months earlier and been told he had the body of a thirty-five year old. Glen had gone for a run early that morning, something that he did two or three times a week. His wife, Mary, was away visiting their daughter, so she didn't even know there was a problem until she received the dreaded phone call.

At the funeral, Jerry felt nervous as he approached her.

"I'm so sorry for your loss. I wish I had found him sooner. Maybe I could have done something to save him."

Mary took his hand and pulled him in close to give him a hug. "It's not your fault", she whispered. "The doctors said he died quite quickly and there's nothing you could have done, but I thank you for trying."

At the funeral, there were numerous people who spoke about Glen. Hockey buddies said he was the kind of guy who would crush you into the boards during a game, but then buy you a beer afterwards. People from the golf course talked about his hours and hours of practice on the range as he perfected his ability to work the ball both ways. Why hit the ball straight when the shot called for a draw or a slight fade to get it close to the pin? He was the captain of their Challenge Cup team and the ultimate leader.

His son spoke about his father – how he loved to coach his hockey and soccer teams, or anything really where there was competition involved. Yet he wasn't a person who believed in the "*win at all costs*" philosophy. Fairness and integrity were traits that would always be associated with his father.

Mary was the last to speak. "Don't feel sorry for Glen. He lived a good life. It was just too short. He said he'd always felt like luck was on his side. In business, in sports – and in love. But I think it was those of us who got to know Glen that were the lucky ones. The last few days were especially good. He got to see our son get his Master's degree and our daughter gave birth to a grandson just three weeks ago."

Mary paused for a few seconds to compose herself before continuing. As she wiped the tears away, she noticed someone sitting in the fourth row of the church.

She smiled at him.

"And Glen was particularly proud that he'd finally managed to defeat Jeff in a round of golf," she said as she pointed at him. Smiles spread throughout the church as people recalled how ecstatic Glen had been when he'd finally beaten his nemesis.

"But let this serve as a wake-up call for all of us," she continued. "Life is precious. It can be taken from each of us in the blink of an eye. Live your life to the fullest each and every day. I know Glen did."

CHAPTER 2:   FIRST TEE JITTERS

Max Wakelam, the head pro at Riverview, was sitting in his office going over the latest financial statements for the club when there was a soft knock on his door. He smiled when he looked up. "Darren, what brings you by?"

Darren Fletcher was the head professional at Blackhawk Ridge, a newer high-end golf course built in the hills overlooking the city. Darren had been Max's assistant pro at Riverview almost ten years earlier. "If you're not too busy, I was hoping we could talk about the Challenge Cup."

"I'd rather talk about anything than look at a bunch of numbers," Max said as he closed the file. "I really appreciate you allowing us to cancel the last day of the Cup this year. With Glen's sudden passing, our members didn't feel it was appropriate to hold the event. He *was* our captain, after all."

"Yeah, our members all agreed. We knew he was the heart and soul of your team."

Max shoved a box containing golf shirts off a chair to give Darren a place to sit. "Besides, you guys were so far ahead in points, you only needed to win three of the singles matches to win the Cup again anyway."

"That's sort of what I wanted to talk about," Darren said. "Some of our members think the competition's become a bit too one-sided and were wondering if it was time to shut it down."

Max was stunned. "But we still raise a lot of money for charity. That's the most important thing, isn't it? Who cares if your club has won it five years in a row?"

"Seven, actually," Darren said. "You guys won it the first two years, but we've won it every year since."

"What brought this on?" Max asked.

Darren refused to look him in the eye. "Some of our members said they're starting to feel guilty – feel like they're beating up on a bunch of senior citizens. Look, the average age of our team is about thirty-five and your team is probably over sixty. It doesn't seem fair."

Max could feel his blood pressure rising. His face was red and his hands were clinched tightly into fists. "I don't want it to end like this," he said. "I don't want the last year of the Challenge Cup to be one where we conceded because of Glen's death." He took a deep breath. "Next year will be the tenth year. We'll put together a competitive team, I promise. If we don't, then we'll shut it down."

Darren still looked nervous. "Look, I'm sorry. I know one of the reasons you started this competition in the first place was to help me get our new course up and running. I'll always be grateful for that."

"Don't start feeling sorry for us," Max said. "You're right. We've probably gotten a little soft over the years, but that ends right now. So I'd suggest you get out of my office and head back to your own club and tell your members to start practicing, because they're going to have to bring their A-game next year. We're not going to just throw in the towel."

* * *

After Darren left, Max spent a long time staring out the window. Suddenly he became aware of his own reflection in the glass. *Where had the guy with the greying hair, the sun-fed wrinkles and the slight pot belly come from?* But then he locked in on the eyes of the person in the reflection. They were still the same – the eyes of a competitor. The same guy who could hit a knock-down four iron into a strong headwind and then make the ten footer for birdie to close out the match.

Max's thoughts were interrupted by another knock on the door. "Hey Boss. There's a guy out here inquiring about memberships. You wanna talk to him?"

Max forced on a big smile. "Absolutely." He headed out of his office and approached a man who was taking a practice stroke with one of the new putters that were on sale. "Hi, I'm Max Wakelam, head professional."

The man placed the putter back in the rack and shook Max's hand. "Ian Martin."

The man looked younger than their typical member and had the tan of someone who spent a lot of time on a golf course. Max invited him into his office.

"Are you purchasing a condo in our community?" Max asked.

"No, I'm afraid the places here are a little out of my price range. You're still allowing non-resident members, aren't you?"

"Yeah, we've still got a few of those spots left," Max said, "but they have some restrictions. We'll be discontinuing them once we get a full membership. They're really trial memberships; it's our way of allowing someone to play here for a year to see if they like the golf course and the community. Most of the people who've had them have decided to move into the community and become full members."

"My situation is a little different," Ian said. "My wife and I are members at Blackhawk Ridge. We separated a few months ago and it's sort of…um…*awkward* for us to play at the same club."

"I'm sorry to hear that," Max said. "I'm divorced myself, so I know what you're going through."

"Maggie and I are just separated so far – not sure where it's going to end up – but we agreed that it's probably best if I play somewhere else next year. I can't afford to fork over another initiation fee at a new club, so here I am."

"Well, I hope things work out between you and your wife, but in the meantime, a guy's gotta have a place to play golf, right?"

"It's the only thing keeping me sane these days." He looked at a picture of the course layout that was hanging beside Max's desk. "I've never actually played here before, so I was wondering if I could get a round in before deciding."

"Absolutely," Max said. "Let's go talk to our starter to see where he can fit you in."

* * *

Mr. Martin stood by the pro shop as Max walked over to talk to the starter. There seemed to be a lot of conversation going on as they flipped the pages back and forth on the tee sheet. Whenever the starter pointed to a potential opening, Max shook his head. *Was this club too exclusive for them to accept him?* He tried to remain calm and not show how desperate he was to be a member of a golf club, or a member of anything else for that matter. Max walked back toward him.

"I didn't mean to put you in a tough spot," Mr. Martin said. "If your tee sheet is full, just fit me in whenever you can. I don't mind waiting."

Max smiled. "Don't worry. I'm sure we'll find you a suitable group to play with. What do you normally shoot?"

"I'm a six handicap, but my game has been a bit off the last few weeks, so don't worry about that. I'll play with anybody who'll take me."

Max thought for a second. "I think I know the perfect group for you. They lost one of the members of their group a few weeks ago. Wait here."

Max approached three guys who were warming up on the putting green.

Mr. Martin felt nervous as they all looked over at him. He wished he'd worn a better golf shirt. He tried to smile, but it seemed fake. They all started walking toward him.

"Mr. Martin, I'd like to introduce you to three of our members who'd be pleased to have you join them," Max said. "This is Ray Ferguson, Bruce Thompson and Jeff Stryker."

"Hi, I'm Ian Martin, but my friends call me Cheech."

"Cheech?" Ray asked.

"Yeah, I picked that up in college. I used to do impressions of *Cheech & Chong*." He could see the strange looks on their faces. "Surely, you've heard of them, right?"

"Yeah, I must have heard their routines a thousand times," Bruce said.

Max watched them banter back and forth for a few minutes. He felt confident that these guys would make

Cheech feel welcome.

* * *

When they made their way to the first tee, all three members hit perfect tee shots, right down the middle of the fairway. Cheech was up next and it was obvious that he was nervous. "You guys are a tough act to follow," he said as he teed up his ball.

First tee jitters are normal, particularly when you know everyone is watching, and this was Cheech's debut. He took a few extra practice swings, but still didn't feel comfortable as he prepared to hit. His shot barely got three feet off the ground as it snap-hooked toward the sand trap. Fortunately, it hit the rake and ricocheted back into the fairway. This was not the start he wanted.

CHAPTER 3: STAYING ON PLANE

Cheech strode down the fairway trying to make it appear that he wasn't bothered at all by his shaky start.

"So what do you do for a living?" Ray asked.

Shit, why do people always start off asking about your job?
"Actually, I'm between jobs right now," Cheech said. "I was the Canadian VP of Sales and Marketing for a car company until a few months ago – when they decided they wanted to go with someone younger."

"Sorry to hear that," Ray said.

"Oh, it's not so bad. Gives me more time to work on my golf game."

"They give you a good package?"

"Not as good as it should have been. I was there almost twenty-five years, twenty-four years and ten months to be exact. I think the bastards let me go just before I qualified for the enhanced pension. My lawyer thinks I've got a really strong case, but it could be years until I get a penny out of them."

Cheech put his bag down when he reached his ball. He was at least eighty yards short of the other drives.

"Any idea what my distance is from here?"

"Not sure," Bruce said with a grin. "I haven't been this far back since I was in the two-ball with my wife."

"Don't be an ass," Ray said.

Stryker walked over and found the nearest sprinkler head which had the distance to the middle of the green marked on it. "It's two-fifteen from here, so you're probably looking at just over two hundred to the left front edge of the green."

The pin was tucked to the right, behind a sand-trap. "So probably two-twenty to the hole," Cheech said.

"Since it's your first time here, I'll let you know that's a sucker pin," Stryker said. "The smart play is to the left side of the green, take the trap out of play and try to two-putt for par."

"No one's ever accused me of being smart," Cheech said as he pulled his five-wood from the bag.

He took aim at the pin and flushed it. It looked perfect, dead-solid perfect, until it suddenly dropped and buried in the lip of the bunker.

"Son-of-a-bitch!" he said. "Thought it was there."

The others didn't say anything, but walked up to their balls. Bruce and Ray each hit the green with their second shots and two-putted for pars. Stryker hit his shot to the left side of the green and had about a fifteen-footer for birdie, but his putt lipped out and hung on the edge of the hole. He glared at it for a few seconds until it finally succumbed to his will and fell in.

Since Cheech's ball was buried in the trap, it took him two shots to get out. Then he two-putted for a double-bogey six.

"Tough start," Ray said as they walked off the green, "but the next one's a birdie hole so you can probably get one back."

"So what do you guys do?" Cheech asked while they waited on the next tee.

"I've been retired for a couple of years now," Ray said. "Used to be in law enforcement." Although Ray was coming up to his sixty-fifth birthday, he took pride in the fact that he still did sit-ups and push-ups every morning after getting out of bed.

Ray nodded toward Bruce. "Bruce was an accountant."

"I still *am* an accountant," Bruce corrected. "Why do people always talk about me in the past tense?"

Bruce was in his early sixties, but the belly hanging over his belt showed that he didn't share Ray's commitment to staying fit.

"Come on," Ray said. "You've been winding down your accounting practice for years now. When's the last time you actually turned on your calculator?"

Cheech turned to Stryker. "How about you?" he asked. "What do you do?"

Stryker was obviously the youngest of the group, but Cheech wasn't sure by how much. He guessed he was probably approaching fifty.

"I'm a lawyer," Stryker said. "Been running a small firm with my partner for over twenty years now."

Stryker had the honours and put his tee in the ground. He was lining up his shot preparing to hit when Cheech whispered to the others. "Sounds like the start of a joke. An accountant, a lawyer and a cop walk into a bar…"

Stryker backed away from his shot and glared at him.

"Sorry," Cheech said.

Stryker regrouped and then tried to hit a draw, but the ball hung out to the right and caught the trap. He slammed his driver back into his bag. Bruce and Ray both hit the fairway with their shots.

E. A. BRIGINSHAW

Cheech hit one of the best drives of his life. The ball landed on the downslope and bounded twenty-five yards past the others. "Got both cheeks into that one," he bragged.

"Whoever sets your pins must have a mean streak," Cheech said when he got to his ball. Once again, it was tucked to the right, behind the sand-trap. A water hazard also bordered the right side.

"If you think you can get there, you should just hit to the left side of the green," Stryker said. "If not, you should probably lay back to about a hundred yards – like we did."

Cheech threw up a bit of grass to gauge the wind. *I think it's about time I show these guys what I'm really capable of.* He pulled a wood from his bag. "Actually, I'm feeling really good about cutting a three-wood in there and cozying it up close to the hole for eagle."

Stryker looked doubtful, but held his tongue.

As soon as Cheech hit his shot, it was apparent that it was heading for trouble. He hit it a little off the toe. It started right of his target and then continued to slice even farther to the right. Splash.

"Damn," Cheech said.

The others just picked up their bags and walked up to their balls. They each hit their wedge shots onto the green, but no one managed to make birdie. Cheech took a penalty shot and dropped a new ball alongside the water hazard, hit a good pitch shot over the trap, but missed the par putt. He was now three over after just two holes.

As they waited to tee off on the third hole, Bruce noticed Cheech was nervously spinning the wedding ring on his finger. "Does your wife play? If she does, the club holds a lot of two-ball events for couples throughout the year."

"She does," Cheech said, "but we're currently separated". He decided not to share the fact that she'd kicked him out when she found out he'd been chasing some young skirt at a convention last year. "She's quite a good golfer and we won a few couples tournaments back at our old club."

"What club did you play out of?" Ray asked.

"Blackhawk Ridge."

Cheech could almost feel the temperature drop as soon as the words were out of his mouth.

"Ah, the enemy," Bruce said. "How do we know you're not here to spy on us?"

Cheech gave them a blank stare.

Ray gave Bruce a sideways glance to encourage him to lighten up. "Bruce is just a little sensitive because Blackhawk Ridge has kicked our ass the last few years in the Challenge Cup." Ray took a closer look at Cheech. "I don't remember seeing you on their team."

"I wasn't," Cheech said. "Back then, I was too busy working to commit to a team, but my wife played on it. She still plays there. That's why I'm looking for a new club."

The third hole was a drivable par-four with a water hazard in front of the tee that extended down the entire right side of the fairway. Stryker hit first and hit a five-iron to the middle of the fairway. Cheech wondered if Stryker ever hit a shot that wasn't the "smart" shot. Bruce hit next and his ball landed in the fairway, about eighty yards short of the green.

"Maybe you could play on our team next year," Ray said after he hit his shot, "assuming you to decide to join our club."

"Hold on," Stryker said. "He'd have to qualify to make the team first." Cheech could tell that Stryker didn't think he was good enough.

"Come on," Ray said. "He's a six handicap. He'd make it easy."

"What do I have to do to qualify?" Cheech asked.

"It's sort of like qualifying for the Ryder Cup," Ray said. "Members of the team are picked on scores they post in qualifying rounds."

"Don't forget about the ladies," Bruce interjected.

"Yeah, right," Ray said. "The ladies do the same thing, so the team ends up with six men and six women."

"Sounds like fun," Cheech said. "I'll probably give it a shot next year."

"Lots of people try," Stryker said, "but some can't handle the pressure."

Cheech took out his driver. He hit it well and it had enough distance to make it to the green, but it hung out to the right and landed in the hazard. He pulled out another ball and prepared to re-tee.

"It's red-staked," Stryker said. "You should take the penalty shot and just drop another ball up there where it entered the hazard."

Cheech ignored the advice. He knew he could make this shot and wanted to prove it to Stryker. This time his drive drew in and landed about twenty yards short of the green, took one big bounce and then rolled onto the green, stopping about a foot from the hole.

"Just a routine par," Cheech said.

* * *

When the four of them added up their scores at the end of the round, Stryker was only two over par and both Ray and Bruce managed to break eighty. Cheech barely broke ninety which included eight penalty shots, four for hitting it out of bounds and another four for hitting it into the numerous water hazards spread throughout the course.

"Sorry I didn't play better," he said.

"Don't worry about it," Ray said. "It was your first time here. It takes a few rounds to figure out where to hit it."

"And where not to," Bruce added.

"I've been struggling with my game for a while now," Cheech said. "I wish I knew what I was doing wrong."

"You're totally off-plane," Stryker said. "Half the time you're laying the club off on your backswing and then coming over the top and pulling it to the left or slicing it to the right."

Jeez, this guy thinks he's an expert in everything. But Cheech knew he was probably right. His whole life was off kilter, so it made sense his golf swing would be as well.

Ray put his hand on Cheech's shoulder. "I'm sure your game will come around. We normally head into the clubhouse for a drink after the round. Care to join us?"

"Thanks," Cheech said, "but I can't. I told the pro I'd stop in to see him."

After the others headed into the clubhouse, Cheech pulled his seven-iron from his bag and started to check his club position at the top of his backswing. He moved closer to the pro-shop so he could see his reflection in the glass window and was surprised to see how out of alignment he was.

Max came out of the pro-shop. "So how did you like our course?"

"The course was great. My game – not so much. I think I might need a lesson to get me back on track. Think you can help me out?"

"I don't teach much myself anymore," Max said, "but we've got a couple of assistant pros who could probably get your game back in shape. Come inside and we'll take a look at their schedules."

As he paged through the bookings, Max saw that Grant, the head teaching pro, was booked up for the next few weeks. The club had recently hired Patti Hoffman, a former LPGA player, who now specialized in teaching. "Patti could fit you in the middle of next week," Max said. "I know some guys don't like taking lessons from a woman, but she's good, really good. She even coaches some of the tour players."

"I don't have a problem with that," Cheech said. "If she can help me get my game back on track, then I'm all for it."

"I'll pencil you in for next Wednesday at ten. Patti will call you to confirm."

"Sounds great," Cheech said. "I presume you want me to write you a cheque for the membership."

"Sure, but since we've only got a few more weeks left in this season, it'll be applied to next year's fees. If you give me a cheque today, we'll let you play here for the balance of this year at no extra charge."

Cheech reached out and shook Max's hand. "Deal."

CHAPTER 4: MID-LIFE CRISIS

Cheech threw his clubs into the tiny trunk of his car. When he tried to slam it shut, his golf bag prevented it from closing. He had purchased the little red sports car on impulse just a few months ago, when the sales lady told him he looked good driving it. Not one of his smartest purchases. He jammed his golf bag in a little further and managed to get the trunk closed on his second attempt. Then he raced over to the Riverview golf course hoping to get there with enough time to get warmed up before the instructor arrived. He was on the range pounding out drives when he heard her approach.

"Good morning. I'm Patti Hoffman. I hear you're having some problems with your golf swing."

Cheech introduced himself and reached out to shake her hand. Before the lesson, Cheech had googled her name and found out that she had played on the LPGA tour for a few years. She was now in her forties, but her athletic build made her seem younger.

"Okay, let's see you hit a few and we'll see what's going on," Patti said.

Cheech sucked in his gut and pounded out a few more drives. The first three he hit were perfect, but he pulled the fourth one and then over-corrected and sprayed the next one to the right.

"Let me see you hit a few with your seven-iron," Patti said.

She stood behind Cheech watching closely while he hit four or five more shots. Then she faced him while he hit a few more. Cheech felt surprisingly nervous and was trying to make sure he didn't lay the club off on his backswing, like Stryker had told him.

She watched him hit almost twenty shots before she spoke. "Okay, I think I see what's going on."

Cheech stopped swinging. He felt like he was waiting for the doctor to give him the bad news that he only had six months to live.

Patti gave him a sympathetic look. "As we get older, we can't do the shoulder turn the way we did when we were younger."

Ouch! Did she just call me old? His jaw dropped and his gut flopped out to its usual positon.

"You're getting across the line at the top, which is going to cause you problems at impact."

"But Stryker told me I was laying the club off," Cheech countered. "I've been trying to fix that."

"Well, now I think you've gone too far the other way. Take your backswing and I'll show you what I mean."

Cheech slowly took his backswing and stopped part-way back. Patti moved in and put one hand on his right shoulder and the other on his left elbow.

"Ideally, you want to keep turning your chest and shoulders to get a full backswing," she said as she tried to pull his arms to a full rotation around his body. "But since you don't have the flexibility you did when you were younger, you're no longer able to fully rotate your body. You're just raising your arms and getting across the line at the top."

There she goes again with the "as we get older" crap. Cheech sighed. "So what do I do about it?"

"If you can no longer fully rotate your chest and shoulders, then you should just shorten your backswing. It'll cost you some distance, but it will improve your consistency. Maybe do some exercises to improve your flexibility."

Cheech hit a few more shots with his seven-iron using a shorter backswing. He was definitely hitting them better and it looked like it was only costing him a few yards in distance. "I'd like to try a few with my driver again."

With the shorter backswing, his drives were going about twenty yards shorter. *I can't afford to lose that much distance.* He tried lengthening his backswing just a little bit.

"Hold on," Patti said. "You're starting to raise your arms again." She moved in behind him and put one hand on his back and the other on his right arm. "If you keep raising your arms independent of your body, your club will start to rotate and you'll get across the line at the top." She pulled up on his arms to demonstrate. "Let's start over from address."

She moved in front of Cheech and put her right hand in the middle of his chest. He became aware of how good she smelled and sucked in his gut again.

"Okay, now slowly take the club back," she said. As he did so, she pushed on the right side of his chest. "It's important that you rotate your chest along with your arms in a connected fashion." She moved to his side and was almost hugging him as she demonstrated the proper turn.

"You smell wonderful," Cheech whispered.

Patti immediately stepped back and gave him a stern look. "I think you just crossed the line again."

Cheech felt his face flush. "I'm sorry. That was inappropriate. I'm sorry. So, so, sorry."

Patti studied his face for what seemed like an eternity before she spoke. "Let's try this a different way." She grabbed the head cover from his driver. "Put this under your right arm." It was like a command from a drill sergeant and Cheech did exactly as he was told. "Now when you take your club back, it's important that the head cover not fall out from underneath your arm. If it does, then it means that you've gone too far and your arms are starting to separate from your chest."

Cheech followed her instructions precisely for the rest of the lesson and Patti didn't come within ten feet of him after their little incident.

After she left, Cheech just stared at the ground. *I am such an idiot. What the hell was I thinking?*

* * *

When Cheech was sorting through his mail later that evening, he was surprised to see three letters in the pile, one from Ford, one from Chrysler and one from Toyota. It had been less than two weeks since he submitted his applications for marketing positions with each of those companies. He was expecting to receive calls requesting that he come in for interviews about now. He opened the letter from Toyota first.

"We have reviewed your experience and qualifications in relation to the position and at this time we will not be proceeding with your application. We will, however, keep your resume on file and consider your qualifications for suitable positions as they become available. We wish you success with your future endeavours."

He read the letter again, and then a third time. It didn't make any sense. The position had asked for more than five years of sales and marketing experience to weed out the junior candidates. He had over twenty. He had a Bachelor of Commerce degree and an MBA. *How much more fucking qualified could I be?*

He opened the letter from Ford, but could instantly tell it was a form letter. Thanks, but no thanks. The letter from Chrysler looked like a photocopy of the one from Ford, but with a different logo and letterhead.

He slumped into his chair. He wondered if he would ever work again. All of these companies complain about not being able to find qualified people. He was more than qualified, yet he couldn't even get an interview.

He pulled a copy of his resume out of his desk drawer and stared at it wondering what the problem was. It detailed all of the successful marketing campaigns he had run over his career. It showed he had graduated from the University of Western Ontario in 1979 and then obtained his Master's degree a few years later. It showed page after page of the positions he had held over the years, progressing from junior positions to middle management, finally leading to a position as a senior vice president of sales and marketing. The first page of his resume showed the same picture of him that had hung on the wall at his old company, along with all of the other executives. He looked smart, distinguished and successful.

And then it hit him.

It also showed how old he was. It looked like the same pictures he saw every day in the newspaper – under obituaries.

He pulled out his laptop and opened the document containing his resume. First, he removed the picture. Then he removed the dates showing the years he graduated and got his MBA. It still showed his education, just without the dates. He left the dates for his most recent positions, but summarized the older ones under a heading of "Prior Positions".

His resume was now down to just three pages. It would look just like all of the ones from applicants in their thirties. Why make it easy for them to move his application into the "too old" pile?

CHAPTER 5:   ONE IS A LONELY NUMBER

Jerry was once again up before daylight, even though he wasn't scheduled to work that day at the golf course. For some reason, he found himself waking up earlier and earlier these days.   He made himself some breakfast, turned on the TV, and sat down in front of it to watch the latest highlights on *"SportsCentre"*. When he realized he was watching the same looped program over and over, he started flipping through the channels until he came to *"The Price is Right"*.   It was one of his favourite shows when he was a kid, but it somehow didn't seem the same without Bob Barker hosting.

He turned the TV off. *It must be almost time for lunch.* He glanced at the clock. *Nope, not even close.* It wasn't even ten yet.

He headed into his den and fired up his laptop to check his email, but there was nothing new in his inbox. He remembered the days at work when he used to get so many emails that he couldn't keep up with them. Now, he actually looked forward to getting those unsolicited emails from vendors inviting him to their online webcasts where they could pitch the latest and greatest features of their products.

But Jerry's work days were done, and good riddance. He didn't have to worry about hitting deadlines and quotas any more. He was now supposed to be living the good life.

He picked up the picture of him and his wife posing in front of the camper-van they had planned to use for their world tour. Well, North America, anyway. The vehicle was over ten years old now and had barely made it out of the driveway. He headed out to the garage and ran a chamois over it, even though he could already see his reflection in it. *I should probably sell it. I'll put an ad in the paper tomorrow.* But he knew he wouldn't.

He headed back inside and made himself lunch, even though it was barely eleven. Then he cleaned the kitchen until it was spotless. She had always liked it that way.

Shortly before one, Jerry headed out to the Shady Oaks Retirement Home where he volunteered several times a week. Sometimes he played cards with the residents, or a game of Scrabble. Other times he would play the piano. He wasn't very good and he only knew four songs, but they didn't seem to mind. His wife was the talented one of the family.

When he arrived, he saw Elena waiting for him just inside the door. Elena was in her forties and coordinated all of the volunteers at the home. They all referred to her as the den mother as she was very protective of the residents and wouldn't stand for any nonsense from the volunteers. But it was obvious she had a bit of a soft spot for Jerry.

"Good afternoon, Jerry. You're right on time, as usual." She turned and waved at two young women to come over. "This is Jessica," she said as she pointed to a blonde girl who looked about seventeen-years-old. "And this is Emily." Emily had jet black hair and looked to be in her early twenties. "Ladies, this is Jerry, one of our longest serving volunteers."

"Ah, you must be the new candy stripers," Jerry said.

Both girls winced at the moniker.

"Junior volunteers," Elena corrected. "Jessica is in her last year of high school and is thinking about going into nursing. Emily is already in nursing school. They'll both be with us part-time."

"Welcome," Jerry said. "I look forward to working with you."

Jerry headed into the main hall, went over to one of the storage cupboards along the wall and pulled out a cribbage board and some cards. He spotted a table with three ladies sitting at it who didn't appear to be doing much of anything. He introduced himself.

"Anyone interested in playing some cribbage?"

"Oh that would be wonderful," one of the ladies said. "I love cribbage." She was one of the younger residents at Shady Oaks and looked to be in her late sixties. Her silver hair had that poofy hairspray look to it that seemed to be prevalent in nursing homes.

"Shirley, you're looking lovely today. Have you been to the beauty parlor?"

She blushed. "Oh, you're too kind. Are you new here?"

One of the other ladies at the table scowled. "Oh, Shirley. You know Jerry. He comes here every week!"

Jerry sat down at the table and started to deal the cards. "Not to worry. Shirley, why don't you and I be partners and see if we can skunk these other two."

The ladies were actually pretty good at cribbage, although Jerry had to help them a few times count up their points at the end of each hand. Jerry and Shirley won two out of the three games, although they didn't come close to skunking the other two. After the third game, Jerry noticed their attention waning.

"Anyone interested in hearing a few tunes?"

He headed over to the old upright piano on the other side of the room and started to play. His first tune was an up-tempo jig that had several of the seniors clapping along. Next, he played a slow waltz and sung the words, although he wasn't a very good singer as they could barely hear him.

"What a lovely song," Shirley said when he finished. "What's it called?"

"The Tennessee Waltz."

"Would you play it again?"

Jerry noticed that she seemed off in her own little world as he played it the second time. Most of the other seniors began to wander off as it was now time for afternoon tea. By the time he was finished, the only one left was Shirley.

Jessica came over and listened to the last few bars of the song. "Shirley, are you going to join us for tea today?"

The interruption seemed to jolt Shirley back to reality. She looked at Jessica with a confused look on her face.

"It's time for afternoon tea," Jessica repeated. "Would you like to join the others?" She helped Shirley out of her chair and escorted her to the dining room.

Jerry gave a heavy sigh as he watched them walk away. Once again, he was left alone.

* * *

Two weeks later, Jessica was standing beside Elena, her supervisor, as they watched the seniors finish their lunch. "Some of these people don't seem to get any visitors," she said. "It's so sad. Why don't their families come to see them?"

"Various reasons," Elena said. "People lead busy lives these days, so it's harder and harder to find the time. Most of our residents have someone come to check on them every week or two, but some of their kids have moved away to other cities, so it can be months and months between visits."

"It's so sad," Jessica repeated. "I haven't seen anyone visit Harold since I started working here, but he seems to sleep most of the time anyway. Shirley seems like such a nice lady and a bit of a social butterfly, but no one's come to visit her either. What's her story?"

"She's an absolute dream," Elena said, "but she's fighting dementia. She's been with us for a few years now and she used to get lots of visitors, but they stopped coming when she didn't even know who they were."

"I noticed that she never remembers my name," Jessica said, "but her family shouldn't just abandon her and leave her here to die."

"It's not our job to judge people," Elena said. "We're just here to make our guests as comfortable as possible."

"But Shirley doesn't even have any pictures of her family in her room," Jessica pleaded. "It's just not right."

Elena turned and took both of Jessica's hands in hers. "We can't start meddling in their personal lives. We're here to take care of them, that's all." Elena could see that she still hadn't convinced her. "If it makes you feel any better, I know for a fact that Shirley's family loves her very much. All of her family pictures have been put away. It's too frustrating for her to look at those pictures every day, realizing that she should know them, but not have a clue who they are."

"They should still come to visit her," Jessica protested. "She's so friendly. She seems happy to meet everyone." Jessica leaned in to whisper. "Have you noticed how she lights up on the days when Jerry is working?"

"Yes, all of the residents seem to like Jerry. But Jessica, I want to make myself perfectly clear. Don't start meddling in their personal lives. Do you understand?"

"Yes, Ma'am." She understood completely, but she did not agree.

* * *

The next day, Jessica placed tea and cookies on the table in front of Shirley.

"Thank you, Jessica," Shirley said.

Jessica smiled. It was the first time Shirley had remembered her name in all of the time she had worked there. She noticed Shirley had a troubled look on her face. "Is your arthritis bothering you today?"

"Same as always," she replied.

Jessica knew that every person in the retirement home suffered from one ailment or another. Some complained constantly, others hardly at all. Shirley fell in the latter category, but Jessica could tell that something wasn't right.

As Jessica carried a tray with empty cups back to the kitchen, she passed by Jerry who was just arriving for his shift.

"Make sure you spend some time with Shirley today. I think something may be bothering her."

She really didn't have to say anything. Jerry always made sure to spend some time with Shirley on every shift.

Jessica was kept busy in the kitchen for about the next half hour. When she came back into the dining room, she headed over to stand beside Elena, waiting for her next assignment. She noticed Shirley in the far corner of the room crying. Jerry was trying to comfort her.

"Oh my God," Jessica said. "What happened? Should I go over to help?"

"No, I think Jerry can handle it," Elena said.

They both continued to watch. Jessica had never seen Shirley so upset.

"I could tell this morning that she was having a bad day."

Elena put her hand on Jessica's shoulder. "Believe it or not, today is actually a good day."

CHAPTER 6:   NOBODY SAID IT WAS EASY

After Ray finished his round of golf that day, his fifth of the week, he walked the short distance to his condo which bordered the eleventh fairway.

"Back so soon?" his wife, Candice, said when she heard him come through the door.

"I missed you too," he said as he reclined into his La-Z-Boy. He noticed some grass had adhered itself to his socks and the back of his legs and brushed it off.

"I just finished cleaning," Candice scolded. "Maybe you should go take a shower."

She came over holding a *Dustbuster* and began vacuuming up the bits of grass that were now on the chair and the area rug surrounding it. She saw a few blades of grass on Ray's legs and started to vacuum those up as well.

"All right, all right," Ray said as he got out of the chair. "You win."

As he stood in the shower, he mumbled to himself. "I feel like a visitor in my own home."

When he was still on the police force, their marriage

had been wonderful. He worked long hours and brought home a pretty good paycheck and she raised their daughter, Amanda, and took care of the house. They had a good social life and treasured their time together. The first year of his retirement had also been good as they had done a lot of travelling together. But since then, he felt like he was constantly in the way and getting on her nerves. She was definitely getting on his.

"Amanda called and said she's coming to visit this weekend," his wife said when Ray walked into the kitchen after his shower.

"Again?"

Ray loved his daughter, but this was the third time she had come to visit them in just over a month.

"I think Doug and her might be having some trouble," Candice said. "She's bringing the kids."

Ray sighed. "We better hide all the good stuff."

Amanda and her husband had two kids, Elizabeth who was ten and Tyler, who was seven. Tyler was autistic.

"I never know what to do with that kid," Ray said. "The slightest thing seems to set him off."

"He'll be fine," Candice said.

Ray looked in the fridge for something to eat and found a plate of cupcakes with a mountain of chocolate icing on them. As he eased the plate out, one of them toppled from the plate and landed on the floor, face down.

"Sorry about that. I'll clean it up."

Candice just shook her head. "Never mind, I'll do it. If you clean it up, I'll just have to do it again anyway."

Ray pulled one of the cupcakes from the plate and slid the rest back into the fridge. "I'll be downstairs in the shop if you need me," he said as he hurried out of the kitchen.

* * *

Ray slowly climbed the stairs to his bedroom. His wife had packed it in an hour ago. It had been a long day. Amanda had arrived earlier that day with the kids and it had been a challenge to keep the chaos under control. The low point had been when Tyler threw a tantrum and started throwing things around the living room. It took them a while to figure out that his fit of rage had been caused by hunger and he calmed down after they gave him something to eat. *That kid is now seven years old. I wonder if he'll ever learn to talk.*

When Tyler was an infant, he seemed perfectly normal. Amanda had started getting concerned when he was about eighteen months old because he seemed to be doing everything so much later than his older sister. But every child was different. Elizabeth had started talking and walking much earlier than the norm, so friends had just told her to be patient with Tyler. They had detected that he had a hearing problem when he was two, so they thought that was the cause of his delayed development. He wasn't officially diagnosed as being autistic until he was three. At first, they disagreed with the diagnosis and had withdrawn into their own protective shell. Her husband Doug was devastated.

Tyler had gone to bed around ten and the house had finally returned to its normal peace and quiet. When Ray opened his bedroom door and saw his wife sitting up in bed with the lamp beside her still on, he sighed. After over thirty years of marriage, he knew that meant she wanted to talk.

"I think you should have a talk with Doug," Candice said as she looked up from the book she was pretending to read.

Ray hated discussions that started with *I think you*

should. They never ended well. "I think we should just stay out of it and let them figure out their own marital problems."

"But Amanda said Doug told her he needs a break from Tyler every few weeks to regain his sanity."

"I can understand that," Ray said.

Candice slammed the book shut. "Are you taking his side?"

"I'm not taking anyone's side. I'm just saying that we shouldn't meddle in their marriage. I can understand him needing a break. Tyler just arrived today and I'm already exhausted."

"But Doug shouldn't just be dumping everything on Amanda."

"I agree. I'm sure she needs a break every now and then too."

Ray turned off the lamp on his side of the bed, fluffed up his pillow and then sighed as he sunk into it. The lamp on his wife's side of the bed was still on.

"I still think you should talk to him," she said.

Although he had turned towards the wall and had his eyes closed, he could still feel his wife's glare burning a hole in the back of his head. A few seconds passed. "I'll think about it," he finally said.

"Good. You do that," she said as she turned off the light.

* * *

The following morning Ray came down the stairs to find his wife preparing breakfast.

"Everything should be ready in about ten minutes," she said. "Amanda's still in the shower."

Ray looked in the living room and saw his granddaughter reading. "Where's Tyler?" he asked.

"He was here a minute ago. I think he's in the kitchen with Grandma."

Ray looked back in the kitchen, but could see that he wasn't there. *Where the hell is he? That kid can get into trouble in a matter of seconds.* Ray raced through the house looking for him in all of the bedrooms and bathrooms.

When he opened the door to the den, he was surprised to see Tyler sitting on the floor working on a puzzle that had been sitting on the corner of the desk. The puzzle was a silver and gold map of the world etched onto small tiles that could be slid up or down, or left or right on the mahogany holder. It was one of the presents that had been given to Ray when he retired, supposedly to keep him amused with all of his newly found spare time. Ray had scrambled the tiles and tried to solve it himself once, but had given up because it took too long.

He watched as Tyler slid the tiles around with amazing speed and could see the map of the world slowly starting to take shape. *How can he be doing this? He can't even talk.*

Amanda came through the door with a towel wrapped around her wet hair. "Is Tyler in here?"

Ray put his finger to his lips to signal for her to be quiet and then pointed to Tyler who was still working on the puzzle. They both watched in amazement. When Tyler finished the puzzle, he turned to them with a contented look on his face and quietly left the room.

"How did he do that?" Ray asked.

"I have no idea," Amanda said. "I've never seen him do anything like that before. But I knew there was more going on inside his head than we thought."

"But how did he know what the map of the world actually looked like?"

Amanda thought for a second. "The globe. He's got a globe in his room at home. He loves to spin it around

40

and watch the colours flash by, but I had no idea he actually knew what it was."

She hugged her father. "Today is such a good day."

CHAPTER 7: FATHER/SON COMPETITION

Bruce's condo was empty when he got home after his golf game, although his wife Marilyn had left him a note on the kitchen counter.

"Gone shopping with the girls. Be back by 4:30." It was signed with *"LYP"* as usual, which was their abbreviation for "Love You Passionately". At the bottom of the note, there was a PS which said *"Josh called and said he booked a tee time for us tomorrow at 3:30."*

Josh was their oldest son and had just entered his thirties. When he was a kid, Bruce loved to wrestle with him and had coached several of his football and hockey teams. Josh was super-competitive and quite a good athlete. Now that he was older, Bruce loved their family golf outings which Josh arranged about once a month. They usually just played nine holes and then had dinner together afterwards at his club. Bruce and Josh preferred to play eighteen, but Marilyn thought nine was plenty, so they normally relented to her wishes.

Bruce and Marilyn also had twin daughters, Paige and Emma, who were almost ten years younger than Josh.

They were the *surprise* babies, conceived after a wild New Year's party. Although Marilyn had always wanted a girl, Bruce had nearly driven into the ditch when she told him she was pregnant with twins. He now cherished them and they used that to their advantage whenever possible. Neither of the girls really liked to play golf, so they would take turns as to who played in their family outings, but they both always came for the dinner afterwards. They weren't going to pass up a meal when their parents were buying.

Josh was a member at Blackhawk Ridge and Bruce wanted to get there early the next day. Their greens were a little firmer and faster than at Riverview, so Bruce wanted to practice his putting before they teed off.

"You guys are too serious," Marilyn said when they got there. "Paige and I will be in the pro-shop looking at clothes. Just call us when you're ready to go."

"Don't you want to go to the driving range to warm up?" Bruce asked.

Marilyn raised one eyebrow. "What do you think?"

* * *

Bruce and Josh were still tied when they reached the seventh hole and it was obvious that Josh was pressing really hard to beat his father. Although his handicap was a couple of shots lower than his Dad's, he'd never beaten him in one of their family outings and it was starting to wear on his nerves.

When they reached the green, Bruce two-putted for his par. Josh had about a ten-footer for birdie. He walked around it several times, looking at it from every possible angle, trying to read the break.

"No rush, but it would be nice if you hit the putt sometime before nightfall," Bruce said.

Josh either didn't hear him, or pretended not to hear him. When he finally hit the putt, it looked like he had made it until it got to about a foot from the hole, then it slid by the low side and continued to run about three feet past. "Gimme?" Josh asked.

"Ooh, it looks like there's still a little meat left on that bone," Bruce said. "I think I'm going to have to make you putt that one out."

"Oh Bruce, just give it to him," Marilyn scolded.

Josh clenched his jaw. "No, I'll putt it."

He studied the break again before striking the putt, even though he already knew the line. When he finally hit it, he powered it through the break and it lipped out.

"One up, with two to play," Bruce said.

Josh won the par-three eighth so they were all tied up as they played the last hole. Once again, Josh was looking at a ten-footer for birdie. Bruce had missed the green and was faced with a tough up-and-down from the green-side rough just to save par.

"Tough break, Dad," Josh said with a grin. "That looks like a pretty nasty lie."

Bruce took out his lob wedge, opened the face so it pointed skyward and took a full swing. The ball popped straight up in the air, landed on the edge of the green and slowly rolled toward the cup. It seemed to pause on the lip of the hole just long enough to tease Josh, before finally falling in.

"I saw that shot once on TV," Bruce said as he picked his ball out of the hole.

Josh thought he was going to win the hole easily and finally beat his father, but now he had to make the putt just to tie. As he studied the line, it was obvious he was rattled and he ended up leaving it a foot short.

"Chalk up another win for the old man," Bruce said.

CHAPTER 8:   TAKING CARE OF MOM & DAD

Max walked out of the pro shop and started heading toward his car, hoping to get home a little earlier than normal today. Since it was late autumn, there were hardly any golfers who teed off after three in the afternoon. The staff should be able to handle anything that came up at this point. He had just unlocked his car door when he heard his name being called.

"There's a call for you," Scott yelled as he hurried toward him.

Max sighed. "Just take a message. I'm sure it can wait until tomorrow."

Scott continued toward him. "It sounds urgent. He said his name was Arthur."

Max looked confused. His father *never* called. Their relationship had been strained for over thirty years. Max continued to show up at all of the normal family gatherings like Thanksgiving and Christmas, but his mother and his sister, Karen, acted as a buffer between him and his dad.

Max started to walk back towards the pro shop with

Scott. "Did he say what it was about?"

"I couldn't really understand him. He wasn't making much sense."

Max sighed. "Welcome to my world. He's well into his eighties now and has been battling health problems for the last few years. My mother spends all of her waking hours taking care of him, but she doesn't normally let him use the phone."

When Max picked up the phone, his father was already talking. "I tried calling Karen, but she's not answering. I don't know what to do. I don't know what to do. I went over to see if Mrs. what's-her-name across the street could help – you know, the one with the yappy little dog – I can never remember her name."

"Dad, Dad, it's Max. What's going on?"

"Oh Max, I'm glad you called. I tried calling Karen, but she didn't answer." His father started to repeat how he had tried to contact the neighbor. "Mitzie, no that's the dog's name. What's the lady's name?"

"Dad, it doesn't matter. What happened?"

"It's your mother. She's fallen."

Max immediately sprang into action. "Dad, I'm going to hang up and dial 9-1-1. They'll send an ambulance. I'm on my way over right now."

His father was still talking when Max ended the call. He dialed 9-1-1 and gave the address of his parents' house which was about a twenty minute drive from the golf course. He raced to his car.

As he drove, he thought about his parents. It wasn't supposed to happen this way. He knew that a call like this would be coming someday, but he thought it would be his Mom calling about his Dad. His father was nine years older than his mother and his health had been declining for years. His mother was the rock, the foundation of their family, the person who had been taking care of all of them forever.

Max arrived at the house just as the paramedics were wheeling his mother out of the house. He raced toward her.

"Mom!"

She was conscious and held out her hand to him. "Oh, you shouldn't have left work. I'm fine."

"What happened?"

"I'm not quite sure," she said. "I was working in the kitchen and the next thing I knew I was lying on the floor and these nice young men were asking me all kinds of questions."

Max turned to one of the paramedics. "Did she have a stroke?"

"We're not sure. She was unconscious when we arrived, but her vitals appear to be stable now. We're not detecting any signs of paralysis, but she's got a nasty bump on the side of her head – probably got that when she fell. We're going to take her into the hospital and they'll be able to figure out what happened."

"Which hospital?"

"University is the closest."

"Okay, I'll follow you there," Max said.

His mother reached out to take his hand. "You don't have to do that. I'm sure I'm okay. You should stay here and take care of your father."

Max hadn't even looked for his father, but then saw him sitting just inside the front door of the house talking, even though there was no one there with him.

"Dad, Dad, come with me to the car. We're going to follow the ambulance to the hospital to make sure Mom is okay."

Max closed the front door – he didn't worry about

locking it – and helped his father into the passenger side of his car. They quickly caught up to the ambulance which was only half a block ahead. They didn't have their emergency lights on or their sirens blaring which gave Max some comfort that his mother was going to be okay.

As they drove, Max used the hands-free controls on his car to call his sister, Karen. She answered on the third ring, out of breath.

"Hi Max. Sorry, but I was just coming in. Been out doing some shopping. What's up?"

"I'm on my way to University Hospital right now."

"Oh my God. Is it Dad?"

"No, it's Mom."

Max heard the gasp on the phone. He continued with the details. "She passed out and fell – we're not sure why, yet – but the paramedics said her vitals are stable."

"Did she have a stroke? A heart attack?"

"Don't know."

"Where are you now?"

"We're on Wonderland Road sitting in traffic, right behind the ambulance. I've got Dad with me."

"Hi Dad," Karen said over the speaker. "I'm sure Mom is going to be okay. How are you doing?"

It was like he didn't hear her. He was talking, mostly to himself, but he wasn't making any sense.

Max inched forward as a few more cars in the left-turn lane got the advanced green light, then stopped. The ambulance was still right in front of them. He was sure that they'd make it through the next time the light changed.

Suddenly, the lights on the ambulance lit up and the sirens shrieked. The traffic stopped and the ambulance navigated its way through the intersection and then raced away toward the hospital.

"Oh my God," Max said.

"What happened?" Karen asked.

"I don't know. The ambulance just turned on its siren and sped away."

Max turned to look at his father who had stopped talking. He was now crying.

* * *

Max sighed and slumped back in the stiff wooden chair in the kitchen of his father's house. His sister, Karen, was keeping busy putting away the dishes and wiping the counters. Their father was asleep in his recliner in the living room, with the Golf Channel playing in the background.

"What are we going to do about Dad?" Max asked.

It was a little over a week since their mother's funeral. This wasn't the first time they'd broached the subject, but they still hadn't resolved anything.

"I've made arrangements for a caregiver to come in next week," Karen said, "but she's only going to be here for a few hours every day during the week." She turned and looked directly at Max. "Dad's still going to need someone to keep an eye on him on nights and weekends."

Max wasn't prepared for this. He knew his mother had happily doted on his father for as long as he could remember. He couldn't imagine him taking care of himself. "What about a nursing home?"

Karen shook her head. "Haven't you heard about some of those places? They're dreadful. You might as well just put him in his coffin right now."

"They're not all like that," Max countered. "Jerry volunteers at Shady Oaks and says it's pretty nice."

Karen glared at him. "And who do you think is going

to pay for that? You got a secret stash I don't know about? Mom and Dad were living on just their pensions and old age security. If they didn't already own the house, there's no way they'd get by."

Karen's raised voice caused their father to stir in the living room. After a few snorts, they heard him return to a gentle snore. Karen lowered her voice to a whisper. "Besides, do you really want to put him there?"

Max had to look away. Even he didn't want to do it. "But we've got to do something."

Karen took a deep breath. "Dad's actually in pretty good shape. He doesn't need a nursing home. He just needs someone to look after the basics, make him meals and make sure he takes his pills when he's supposed to."

"And doesn't burn the house down," Max added.

"You're never going to let that go, are you," Karen snapped. "That was just one time when he left one of the burners on the stove on. Hell, I've even done that myself."

"Well, if Mom hadn't smelled the dish towel burning and come racing into the kitchen to put it out, the whole place could have gone up in smoke."

"Well Mom's not here anymore, is she?"

Max heard Karen's voice start to crack. She turned away and looked out the kitchen window while she tried to compose herself. "I can stay with him on weekends," she said in a weak voice. "Can you sleep over here during the week?"

Max's relationship with his father had always been a bit testy, but he knew he had to step up. "I can once the course closes for the winter." That was about ten days away. Over the winter months, Max worked reduced hours from ten to three as there wasn't much to do – taking inventory, preparing budgets, and ordering supplies for the coming year. "But I won't be able to do it once golf season starts up again."

Karen's face showed a glimmer of hope. "Let's not borrow our problems from the future. We'll deal with that later. Let's just get him through the winter."

CHAPTER 9:   OLD VERSUS NEW

Cheech was on the driving range trying a few things to incorporate a shorter backswing without losing any distance on his drives.   He wasn't on the range at Riverview; he was afraid to go back there in case he ran into Patti Hoffman again.   He felt so stupid and embarrassed about making a pass at her.   Maybe all would be forgotten over the off-season.

Cheech was practicing at a range on the outskirts of town.   It was a top-notch facility incorporating multiple target flags at specified distances and a separate area to practice the short game.   Since it was almost the end of the golf season, there were only a few people out practicing, mostly people planning to head south for the winter.

Cheech had strengthened his grip and was trying flatten his swing to gain more power.   He was really struggling with it and snap-hooked another drive.   "Son of a bitch!"

"You know the game is supposed to be fun and relaxing," a man said as he came up behind him.

Cheech turned and saw that it was Bob, the owner of the range. Bob had been the head professional at a few clubs in town over the years and had opened the range after he retired.

Cheech felt his face flush. "Sorry about the language. I didn't realize anyone was close enough to hear."

Bob shrugged. "I've said worse myself. Sometimes the game can get frustrating. Getting ready to head south?"

"No, I'm stuck here for the winter. Just trying to change my swing to get some more power."

"Not possible," Bob said. "You might be able to tweak it a bit, but your swing was pretty much defined after the first ten times you played the game. You're stuck with it now."

"But they say Tiger's gone through three different swing changes."

"Has he really? How's that worked out for him?"

Cheech knew the former number one golfer in the world wasn't even ranked in the top hundred these days. "I see your point, but I've got to do something. I've been told that I've lost some flexibility over the years."

"Haven't we all. Who told you that?"

"Patti Hoffman. She's a pro out at Riverview."

Bob knew who she was and raised an eyebrow. "She knows her stuff. Did she really tell you to change your swing?"

Cheech looked at the ground. "Not quite. She just told me to shorten my backswing."

"So let me guess, that was something you didn't want to hear."

"I suppose not," Cheech said.

Bob moved around in front of Cheech. "When your golf game goes off the rails, it's usually best to go back to the basics – grip, stance and alignment. Let me see you hit a few with your normal swing, not your so-called *new* one."

Cheech hit about four or five shots.

"There's nothing wrong with your swing," Bob said, "so there's no reason to change it."

"But I'm losing distance," Cheech protested.

"Then you'll have to adapt. Instead of hitting an 8-iron into the green, hit a seven, but don't change your swing. Adapt, don't change."

"I suppose you're right," Cheech admitted.

"I'd give the same advice to Tiger if he was here. There's nothing wrong with his swing. But with his back issues and knee issues, he can no longer swing as hard as he did when he was twenty. The sooner he accepts that, the quicker he'll get back on track. Conditions change constantly, both on the golf course, and in yourself. You have to adapt to those changes or you're doomed."

"Thanks," Cheech said.

He watched as Bob walked away. Then he started hitting shots with the same swing he'd had since he was a kid. It felt natural. It felt right.

Bob stopped and turned to watch him. "And remember, the game is supposed to be fun."

* * *

Cheech stared at the huge display of clubs along the wall in the massive golf store. There were clubs from Adams, Titleist, Nike, Ping, TaylorMade and several others, all promising to hit the ball longer and straighter.

"Do you see anything you'd like to try out?" a fresh-faced kid said as he approached. It was apparent that he worked there because he wore the same bright-orange golf shirt worn by all of the staff.

"I'm just looking," Cheech said.

"This is our most popular driver," the kid said. "Just came out. It's got a low CG, the latest speed-slot technology and it's fully adjustable, so we can adjust it if you tend to hook or slice the ball."

"Low CG?"

"Low Centre-of-Gravity. It gives you a higher launch angle and reduces the spin rate."

"And that's a good thing?" Cheech asked.

"Absolutely," the kid said. "Why don't you give it a try in our simulator in the back. It'll tell you exactly how far you hit it. I'm sure you'll gain at least ten yards over whatever you've got now. Guaranteed."

Cheech looked at the price tag. It cost almost as much as he had paid for his last set of irons, all ten of them.

"I don't know," Cheech said. "It's a little pricey."

"Give it a try," the kid said. "What have you got to lose? I'll just tape up the face and meet you back at the simulator."

Cheech watched as the kid raced off. He knew they taped up the face of the club so there wouldn't be any marks left on the club after the "test drive". As he scanned the wall of clubs, he noticed two other drivers from the same manufacturer, both costing significantly less than the model he was about to try. He grabbed both of them and headed back to the simulator.

"I think I'd like to try these two as well, for comparison," he said to the kid.

"No problem. But I'm sure you're going to like this new one. It's sweet."

Cheech hit a few shots with the new club. According to the monitor, it *was* going a little further than his current driver, but not enough to justify spending all that money.

"Really give it a rip," the kid said.

Cheech swung as hard as he could and his next shot did go about twenty yards farther, but it was off-line to the right by about thirty yards.

"Don't worry about that," the kid said. "I'll adjust the weights to produce a draw. That'll add even more yards to your distance."

He took the club from Cheech and was about to move the weights on the bottom of the club, but couldn't find the right tool. He dashed off to find it.

While he was gone, Cheech started hitting some shots with one of the less expensive drivers. They were going about the same distance.

"Is someone looking after you?" someone said from behind him.

Cheech turned to see a silver-haired sales clerk. The bright-orange shirt looked completely out of character on him. His name tag said he was Brian.

"Yeah, he went off to look for something to adjust the weights on the driver," Cheech said.

Brian started to head off to help another customer.

"But since you're here," Cheech said, "can you tell me why this driver is so much cheaper than the other one?"

"It's last year's model. The price always drops when the new model comes out – sort of like cars."

"Is there much difference between them?"

Brian moved in a little closer and lowered his voice. "Sometimes, but in this case, not much at all. It's mostly marketing."

Dave watched him hit a few shots and then moved over to look at the monitor.

"Do you normally hit a stiff shaft?"

"Yeah, I have for the last twenty years," Cheech said. "Why?"

"With your swing speed, you should probably go back

to a regular shaft." He reached into a huge bin of clubs and pulled out the same model that Cheech was hitting and checked the label. "Here, try this one. It's got a regular shaft."

From the first swing, Cheech could tell that it felt right. Even with his normal swing, the ball seemed to be rocketing off the club face.

"How much is this one?" Cheech asked.

"The same price as the cheaper one you were trying, less twenty percent because it's a demo."

"Sold," Cheech said.

Just then, the kid showed up with the expensive driver. "I finally found the tool to move the adjustable weights," he said.

"Never mind. I think I've decided to go with this one," Cheech said as held up the demo model.

The kid glared at Brian.

"Don't worry," Brian said as he started to walk away. "You'll get credit for the sale. And you even sold him the right club for his needs this time."

* * *

Cheech stared at the number calling on his cell phone, but it wasn't one he recognized. *Probably just a telemarketer.* He decided to let it go to voice-mail. A few seconds later, his phone buzzed to let him know he had a new message.

"Hello, this is Dave Hammond calling from Hyundai Canada. Mr. Martin, we received your application and we were wondering if you'd be able to come in for an interview on Wednesday morning at ten."

Cheech excitedly listened to the rest of the message and quickly jotted down the telephone number he was supposed to call. He had sent his modified resume to this company making it less obvious how old he was. He took a few minutes to compose himself and then called the number. Unfortunately, he only got Mr. Hammond's assistant who simply confirmed the time and location of the meeting.

After he hung up, Cheech thought about his last day at his old company. Sales were down, expenses were up, and they had all been tasked to come up with strategies to turn things around. He had been through it all before, several times in fact, as car sales seemed to follow cycles. He had come up with a few good ideas and was looking forward to presenting them to his boss and the rest of the executives.

His boss had asked to meet with him privately half an hour before the scheduled meeting. That's when Cheech was told his services were no longer required. The company wanted to bring in someone with younger, fresher ideas.

"But you haven't even heard my ideas yet," Cheech protested.

"I'm sorry," his boss said. "It's already been decided."

Cheech was escorted from the building like he'd been caught stealing. They told him they would pack up his personal belongings and send them to him. He felt shock, then embarrassment, then anger.

How could they reject his ideas if they'd never even bothered to hear them? It hurt him to the core to hear that they thought he was part of the problem, that the best thing he could do to help the company turn things around was to simply go away.

He never got to say goodbye to the team of people he had worked with, many for over twenty years. A few called later to express their surprise and condolences. But not many. It was amazing how quickly some of them wanted to distance themselves from him, as if he had some kind of contagious disease.

* * *

The following Wednesday, Cheech dressed in his best suit and headed off to the interview. The receptionist showed him into one of their boardrooms and offered him coffee.

The first person to arrive was Martha Johnson, the head of the personnel department. She looked to be in her fifties, although her stylish makeup and clothes took at least ten years off her age.

"Mr. Hammond is running a little late," she said, "but he should be joining us shortly. Did Mr. Hammond explain to you on the phone the type of interview we'll be conducting today?"

"No," Cheech said. "We never actually spoke – just traded messages."

"Are you familiar with behavioural interviews?"

Cheech was not a big fan of them. They had started using them at his old company, but back then, he was the one asking the questions, not answering them. "Yes, I'm familiar with them."

"Good," she said. "They seem to throw some people off if they're not used to them."

Just then, the boardroom door opened and Mr. Hammond came through holding a stack of files in his hand. Cheech was surprised to see that Mr. Hammond was dressed quite casually in an open-collared shirt and looked to be in his early thirties. He quickly looked down at the resume he was holding and seemed confused, as if he had picked up the wrong file.

"Are you Ian Martin?" he asked.

"Yes," Cheech said as he rose to shake his hand. "Nice to meet you."

The interview started off with them asking him to briefly walk them through his work history.

"Very impressive," Mrs. Johnson said. "You've run a lot of successful marketing campaigns over the years."

"Yes, I think we did a case study on one of them back when I was in university," added Mr. Hammond. "It says you graduated from Western. What year was that?"

"1979," Cheech replied.

He saw Mr. Hammond's eyes grow large. *Yes, that's right. Probably before you were born.*

"I completed my MBA in eighty-one," Cheech added.

"Yeah, I never bothered with that," Mr. Hammond said. "Business has changed a lot since the eighties."

Cheech felt the sting of the put-down, but put on a brave face and just smiled.

"Maybe we should move on to the second part of the interview," Mrs. Johnson said.

She asked him a series of behavioural-type questions, questions asking him to describe times he was part of a team, times he led campaigns, and times he had overcome obstacles. He answered the questions flawlessly and he could tell Mrs. Johnson was impressed. But being in sales for his whole career, Cheech knew how to read the room. He had won over Mrs. Johnson, but she wasn't the decision maker. Mr. Hammond was, and he was barely paying attention.

Afraid I'm more qualified than you and going to take your job?

When the interview was over, everyone smiled and shook hands. Mrs. Johnson promised they'd get back to him with a decision within a couple of weeks. But Cheech already knew what the decision would be. Thanks, but no thanks, and best of luck in your future endeavours.

CHAPTER 10: TRYING NEW WAYS

Ray and Candice watched their grandkids, Tyler and Elizabeth, splashing in the water at the indoor waterpark. Everyone was having such a good time. Their daughter, Amanda, was holding hands with her husband, Doug, and they were both hovering close to their kids to make sure they were safe.

"It's nice to see everyone so happy," Candice said. "I'm glad you had a talk with Doug. What did you say to him?"

"Nothing," Ray said. "I told you I wasn't going to meddle. They've got to work things out themselves."

"But I thought you went out for a beer with him last week. What did you talk about?"

"The Jays and whether they're going to win the pennant this year."

Candice did not look happy with his answer. But Ray ignored her glare and headed out towards the water.

"We should probably leave in about twenty minutes," he shouted to Amanda, Doug and the kids. "It's almost supper time."

Amanda waved. "Okay, Dad."

It was just at that moment that another kid accidentally bumped into Tyler sending him backwards into the water. He was only submerged for a few seconds before Elizabeth pulled him back up, but Ray could see the panic on his face. Tyler started to scream and thrash in the water. Doug raced over to try to calm him down, but Tyler continued screaming and fighting him off.

The lifeguards blew their whistles and everyone stopped to watch what was going on. Tyler continued to shriek. It was Elizabeth who finally managed to get him to calm down.

"You should do something to control that kid," a man said to Doug as they walked out of the water.

Doug turned to confront the man and started to walk toward him. Fortunately, Ray was close enough to intervene and stepped in front of him. He could tell that Doug was both embarrassed and angry.

"Just let it go," Ray said. "He's just being an ass."

He steered Doug back towards their towels and lawn chairs. They started gathering up their stuff to head home. On the way, they picked up pizza. Everyone loved it, especially Tyler.

It was shortly after supper that Tyler started to get agitated again. No one could figure out what the problem was. He'd been fed. It wasn't that late and he didn't seem over-tired, but something was obviously bothering him. Finally, it escalated into another screaming fit.

"I can't deal with this," Doug said to Amanda. "I'm sorry, but I've just got to get out of here."

He grabbed the car keys and bolted for the door.

"You can't just leave every time things get rough," Candice yelled at him.

"It's okay, Mom," Amanda said. "Let him go."

"But he shouldn't just dump everything on you all the time," Candice protested.

"Mom, I can't deal with you right now. I have to take care of Tyler."

Candice didn't want to let it go, but Ray pulled her back. "Not now," he whispered to her.

It took them over an hour to figure out what was bothering Tyler. It was actually Elizabeth who solved it.

"He keeps pulling at his right ear," she said.

They took him to a walk-in clinic and sure enough, his ear had become plugged. The doctor drained his ear and gave them a prescription for some antibiotics.

* * *

The following morning Ray was fully reclined in his La-Z-Boy chair, trying not to fall asleep. Tyler had woken up early and Ray had volunteered to keep an eye on him while Candice and Amanda slept.

Elizabeth was also awake and was sitting on the couch listening to music through the earbuds connected to her iPad. Tyler sat beside her, watching her every move. It was obvious he adored his sister.

"Is it okay if I get something to eat?" Elizabeth asked her grandfather.

"Sure," Ray said. "There's cereal in the cupboard to the right of the fridge."

Since Elizabeth was ten, Ray felt comfortable that she could handle everything herself. She put her iPad on the coffee table before heading into the kitchen.

After she left, Ray watched as Tyler picked it up. He placed one of the earbuds in his ear, the one that wasn't hurting, and then started scrolling through the list of songs on the device.

Tyler would listen to the start of a song and then

pause it if he didn't like it, before choosing a different song. When he found a song he liked, he would listen to it two or three times before choosing the next one. *This kid is amazing.* He seemed to have no trouble at all figuring out where to push or swipe on the device. *And this was a kid that couldn't even talk yet.*

It reminded Ray of a feature he had seen on "60 Minutes" a while back, about how some autistic people were now using technology to help them with everyday tasks. He pulled his cellphone out of his pocket and wondered whether he still had the number for the lady from Social Services in his list of contacts. There it was. It was still only eight-thirty in the morning, but he decided to call anyway. She answered on the second ring.

"Ray, it's been a while. I thought you retired."

Ray knew Sarah from his days as a cop. She had always come through for him if he needed help with an abandoned or abused child.

"I did," Ray said. "This isn't police business. It's personal."

This caught Sarah by surprise. "Personal? What's up?"

"Remember that autistic kid that we pulled out of a home a few years ago?"

"Yeah, Danny Carson. I hear he's doing quite well these days. What about him?"

"It's not really about him, but I remember he couldn't talk and you brought in some device to the station to help us communicate with him. Do you still have that thing?"

"I'm sure we do, but there's better technology available these days. That thing is pretty old now."

"Do you think I could borrow it?" Ray asked.

"I suppose," Sarah said, "but I'm not sure you'd be able to figure out how to use it. It's pretty complicated.

Who's it for?"

"My grandson. He's autistic – can't talk – but I'm starting to think something like that might be able to help him."

"How old is he?"

"Seven. Is that too young?"

"No, that's just about right," Sarah said. "Give me a sec," she said as she put him on hold. It was almost a minute later when she came back on the line. "Tell you what, how about I come by your place tomorrow at lunch. I'll bring the device with me – actually, a newer version – and we'll see if your grandson is a suitable candidate. How does that sound?"

"Perfect," Ray said. "See you then."

As he hung up the phone, he heard the squeak of the back door.

"Hi, Dad," Elizabeth said.

Ray couldn't hear the rest of their conversation as they whispered to each other. After a minute or two, Doug slowly entered the living room.

"You must hate me," Doug said.

"Not really," Ray said. "Hate is a pretty strong word. I can tell you're frustrated."

As a former cop, Ray had been in a lot of living rooms dealing with domestic situations. He knew the key was to remain calm.

Doug sat on the end of the couch and looked at Tyler, who seemed completely unaware that he was even there.

"When he throws one of his fits and I can't get him to stop – sometimes, sometimes, I feel like hitting him," Doug confessed. He looked at Ray. "That's why I run. I just can't handle it, so I run. You must think I'm a terrible father. I know I do."

"You're in a very difficult situation. That's why I think

you need some help. I called a friend of mine from social services."

Doug shot up from the couch. "You called social services? Look, I've never hit him, not once. I swear. You had no right to do that!"

Just then, Amanda came down the stairs. "What's going on?"

"Your father called social services," Doug said. He was now pacing back and forth.

Amanda looked at her father. "Dad?"

Ray got out of his chair and went over to hug his daughter. "Both of you calm down. It's not what you think."

He led her over to sit on the couch and waved for Doug to sit down beside her. Tyler seemed oblivious to the whole situation, but Elizabeth had heard the commotion and come in from the kitchen.

"It's okay," Amanda said. "You go back in the kitchen."

Elizabeth looked at each of them before returning to the kitchen. Ray was sure she'd be listening to everything that was said, even from the other room.

"It's a friend of mine," Ray started to explain. "She's got some kind of a gizmo they use to help communicate with autistic kids. I've seen her use it and it seems to work."

Doug and Amanda looked at each other, each trying to overcome their skepticism.

"Doug, I know you're frustrated that you can't communicate with him," Ray continued. "Think how frustrating it is for Tyler. And look, he already seems to know how to use some of this tech stuff."

Doug looked over at Tyler and saw him playing with the iPad. "That's Elizabeth's. He's not supposed to touch it. He'll break it."

He started to move to take it away from Tyler, but Amanda grabbed his arm to stop him.

"It's okay, Dad," Elizabeth said. She had been watching everything by peering around the corner from the kitchen. "I let him play with it all the time."

"Look," Ray said. "You don't have to do this all on your own. There are people out there who can help you. All you have to do is ask."

* * *

The next day, Sarah Caldwell arrived as expected and spent a few minutes talking to everyone in the living room. "This doesn't work for everyone," she warned, "so I don't want you to get your hopes up, but we've had a few real successes with it." She pulled an iPad from her briefcase, one that was only a little bit bigger than the one Elizabeth had.

"That's not the same device you had before," Ray said.

"That thing was too big, too expensive and almost two years old," Sarah said. "In the tech world, two years is a lifetime."

"I'd like everyone to stay out here while I work with Tyler," Sarah said to the group. She held out her hand to Tyler. "Tyler, why don't you come with me into the kitchen?"

Tyler held his arms tight to his body.

"It's okay," Elizabeth said. She took Tyler's hand and led him into the kitchen.

"Maybe you could join us," Sarah said to Elizabeth, "until he feels more comfortable."

While Sarah, Tyler and Elizabeth worked in the kitchen, the rest of the family waited in the living room. Every few minutes, one of them would begin pacing and attempt to eavesdrop on the proceedings in the kitchen, but they couldn't get an inkling one way or another on how they were doing. After well over an hour, Sarah came into the living room.

"We'd like you to join us," she said.

After everyone had gathered around, Sarah nodded to Elizabeth who helped Tyler get started with the demonstration. She moved his hand over the screen of the iPad and Tyler pushed one of the squares.

"My – name – is," the iPad announced in a digitized voice.

Tyler pushed on another square which opened up a new screen showing pictures of each of them. Elizabeth had helped upload some of their pictures onto the device. Tyler looked at all of the pictures until he found his own. When he pressed on it with his finger, "Tyler" was heard over the speaker.

Next, Tyler swiped the iPad and clicked on a different square. "I – am," the device said. Tyler opened another folder and pressed hard on the screen. It didn't work, so he pressed again and again. He started to get agitated.

"Gentle," Elizabeth said as she placed Tyler's finger on the square.

"Hungry," the speaker announced.

Tyler swiped again. "I – want – some," the speaker said. He quickly opened another folder which showed pictures of different types of foods. He scrolled until he found the picture of what he wanted.

"Grapes," the speaker said when he clicked on the picture.

He clapped his hands excitedly and was grinning from ear to ear. He looked up to see everyone watching in amazement.

"Oh my God," Amanda said as tears streamed down

her face. "He can talk."

* * *

Later that night, Ray slowly headed up the stairs to bed. It had been a long day. When he opened the bedroom door, his wife's bedside lamp was still on.

"I'm glad you told Doug what he needed to do," Candice said.

"I didn't," Ray said. "I have no idea what he needs to do, but I could tell that he was overwhelmed. All I told him was not to be afraid to ask for help. It's going to take a whole team of people to help them raise Tyler."

Candice reached over and stroked Ray's back. "I'm sure you helped them a lot today."

"I hope so."

CHAPTER 11: CHANGING TEAMS

Jeff Stryker sat in the boardroom of his law office surrounded by boxes and boxes of files. He normally worked in his own office which was quite large and well appointed, but he'd commandeered the boardroom when the civil litigation case he and his partner had taken on had grown ten-fold.

His partner, Tom Borden, came in and pulled up a chair. "We need to talk," he said.

Stryker didn't even look up. "About what? Never mind, it doesn't matter. I won't have any time for at least ten months."

"That's what I want to talk about."

Stryker pulled another file from the box. "What do you mean?"

"We're in over our heads," Tom said. "We need help."

Stryker still didn't look up. "We'll be fine. We'll just hire a few junior associates to help out."

"I've received an offer from Higgins."

This time Stryker looked up. "What kind of an offer?"

"They want both of us to come work for them."

Higgins, Miller & Tremblay was a huge law firm with about four hundred lawyers distributed over eight offices across the country.

"But we said we'd never sell out to one of the big firms," Stryker said. "There's always been just the two of us, taking cases and going up against the big insurance companies. We're good at it."

"I know," Tom said, "but this case is getting too big. It'll put us in our graves."

The file had started small, representing two patients who had developed severe complications from a new drug. Stryker had done a lot of research on it, all on a contingency basis, and discovered several other patients with the same complications. The two original claims had now grown to eighteen.

"But what about our work, our clients?" Stryker asked.

"Higgins says they've got over thirty similar cases and they're adding more every day. It may go class-action."

Stryker put his elbows on the table and rubbed his forehead as he thought.

"Higgins knows that you know more about this case than any of their lawyers," Tom continued. "They want both of us to join their firm. You'd be made senior partner in charge of all of these files and they have the resources to put as many more lawyers and paralegals on it as you think you need."

"We'd have to make sure our clients don't get lost in the shuffle," Stryker said. "We owe it to them."

"I agree. And with you in charge, you'd be in a position to guarantee that they're still taken care of."

Stryker continued to rub his forehead. "What are they offering?"

"Full partnership for both of us and they're willing to pay a premium for our client list. We can bring all of our staff. They have better health and insurance benefits than we do." Tom decided to play one last card to sweeten the pot. "Partners automatically get full golfing privileges at any of the GolfCorp clubs across the country, including Blackhawk Ridge right here in town."

Stryker continued to struggle with the decision. "I thought it would always be just the two of us in our own little firm taking on the world. I never thought we'd sell out to a big law firm."

* * *

Stryker stood outside the glass walls of the main boardroom at Higgins, Miller & Tremblay looking in at the team of four associates and three paralegals that had been assigned to the class-action lawsuit. His team. The team of people he'd been tasked to lead when he and his partner, Tom Borden, had agreed to merge their two-man practice into the HMT mega-firm. Merge was the polite word they had used in the press release; swallowed would be the more accurate term.

He had no idea what he was going to say to them. He was a shark, someone who was used to hunting and killing on his own, not leading and motivating a team toward a common goal. Although he and Tom had been partners in their old firm, they had followed an "*eat what you kill*" approach that had always worked well for both of them.

"I don't think I've ever seen you look nervous before," Tom said as he came up and stood beside him.

"This may have been a mistake," Stryker confessed. "I can't lead this team. I don't even know half their names. They're going to think I'm a bit of prick."

"You *are* a bit of a prick," Tom said. "That's why you're a good litigator. Just focus on the law and tell them what you need them to do to win the case. That's what they brought us in for."

Stryker gave him a sideways glance. "You really think I'm a prick?"

"Absolutely," Tom said. "Now get your ass in there and take charge."

Stryker watched as Tom walked away. Then he took a deep breath and walked into the boardroom, dropped the dozen files he had tucked under his arm on the table, and took a quick look at the faces surrounding it.

"You, Tall-Guy, I need you to contact the people in these two files and get statements from them before the end of tomorrow." He slid the file folders across the table at him.

"You, in the yellow dress, I need you to do the same on these three files."

"Vanessa, I'm Vanessa Armstrong, second year associate," the girl in the yellow dress said.

Stryker didn't acknowledge her, but looked at the remaining two associates. "You two can divvy up the rest of these files whichever way you like, but I need statements by the end of next week. There's some travel involved."

Then he looked at the three paralegals who were now cowering at the end of the table. "And if you three want to follow me, I've got several boxes of files in my office. I'll need you to organize all of the information in them into a database of some sort so I can pull it up whenever I need it."

Stryker did a quick scan of the faces in front of him. "Any questions?"

No one said a word.

* * *

Max Wakelam was just about to leave the pro shop when his phone rang. Since the golf course was now closed for the winter and the assistant pro was off at a trade show in Phoenix, Max was the only one there.

"Riverview Golf Course, Max Wakelam speaking."

"Hi Max. Jeff Stryker. I wasn't sure if you'd still be there."

"Hi Jeff. I was just getting ready to lock up for the day. What can I help you with?"

Stryker took a deep breath. "I thought I should let you know I won't be coming back to Riverview next year."

"Sorry to hear that," Max said. "Moving somewhere?"

"No. I thought you might have already heard that I've moved my practice over to Higgins, Miller & Tremblay."

"Congratulations. That's a big firm. More money?"

"Maybe, maybe not. But one of the perks at HMT is that I get an automatic membership at the GolfCorp clubs."

Max knew what that meant and felt like he'd been hit in the gut. "So you'll be playing at Blackhawk Ridge."

"Yeah, that's the local club, but they've also got courses in Toronto, Calgary and B.C."

Max was trying to hide his disappointment. "Sounds like a sweet deal."

"It is, but I'd just like to say that I've really enjoyed all of my years at Riverview. It's a great course and I'd recommend it to anyone."

"Thanks, we're proud of it. And thanks for calling to let me know. Good luck at your new club – and your new firm."

After he hung up the phone, Max slumped back into his chair. *How am I ever going to replace Stryker?*

CHAPTER 12: GETTING HELP

Max headed to his father's house after leaving the golf course. He was surprised to find there was no one there, neither his father nor Sylvia, the home-care worker they had hired to look after him for a few hours every day. Through the kitchen window, he could see a light on in the garage and headed out to investigate. He found his father kneeling by the back tire of his old Chevy Impala, cursing a blue streak.

"Dad, what are you doing?"

"What the hell does it look like I'm doing? Never seen a man change a tire before?"

"Dad, you shouldn't be doing that. Where's Sylvia?"

"I sent her home. I can take care of myself. Don't need a baby-sitter checking up on me every five fuckin' minutes."

Max sighed. He could tell his dad was having one of his good days, which unfortunately also meant that he was his ornery, pain-in-the-ass self. "Dad, remember we talked about this. You said you'd let Sylvia help out during the day while Karen and I are at work. She's just here to help."

"I don't need any help. I can take care of myself just fine. You know, I caught her snooping through your mother's stuff. She's got no business doing that. Probably stole something."

"I don't think so," Max said. "I'm sure she was just trying to clean the place up a bit. Remember, you agreed that you'd let us help you out whenever you need it."

His father slammed the tire iron onto the garage floor as he tried to get up from his knees. "Okay, you want to help? Help me change this tire. I can't get the bolts loose – probably rusted on."

Max grabbed his father's arm and helped him up. He saw his father grab his back and wince as he tried to straighten up. "Okay, I'll help. Where's the jack?"

"In the trunk, where it always is," he snapped.

Max reached into the trunk, pulled out the jack and placed it under the back of the car. He put the tire iron into the slot and started to turn it to raise the car.

"You're going to want to loosen the bolts before you lift the car up," his father said. "Haven't you ever changed a tire before?"

Max thought for a second and then realized he probably hadn't changed a tire in over twenty years. "Don't you have CAA?"

"Yes, but a guy shouldn't have to call them just to change a tire. Should be able to do some things yourself."

"Yeah, well I can see you've got a nail in the tire, so they'll probably be able to fix it right here rather than having you drive on that crappy little spare."

Max opened the glove box and rooted through all of the stuff inside until he found the CAA folder. He called them using his cell phone and gave them the membership number.

"They said they'd be here in about thirty minutes," Max said. He could see his father was getting tired. "Why don't we head back into the kitchen and wait there. I'll make you a cup of tea."

They made their way into the kitchen and Max put the kettle on. He looked through the cupboards until he found the package of Earl Grey.

"Are you supposed to be driving?" Max asked while they waited for the tea to steep.

"Of course I am. Why wouldn't I?"

Max poured the tea. Karen had told him about the notice requiring their father to take another test to get his driver's license renewed. Max doubted his father would pass this time, but there was no way he was going to give up his car keys until then.

"Where were you going in the car?" Max asked. "You know, Karen or I can take you anywhere you need to go."

His father gave him a funny look. It was obvious that he'd forgotten where he was planning to go.

"It's not important," his father said as he looked into his tea cup.

* * *

Jerry headed into Shady Oaks for his fifth shift of the week. Since the golf course was closed for the winter, he had the time available to put in more hours as a volunteer at the nursing home. He was standing with Elena, the supervisor of the home, watching all of the patrons taking part in various crafts. Most were gluing small coloured stones onto brooches. One of the staff members was telling them they would make great Christmas presents. A few ladies sat in a circle, knitting.

On the far side of the room, a man in a wheelchair was

painting a picture of a tree they could see through the huge windows along the south wall of the room. Most trees had lost their leaves weeks ago, but there was one maple tree that was being particularly stubborn about giving up its huge coat of red.

Over in the corner, all by herself, Shirley was working on a puzzle. Suddenly, she swept her arm across the table sending all of the pieces onto the floor.

"Something's wrong," Jerry said. He started to head over to her, but Elena put her arm out to stop him.

"Give her a few minutes," Elena said.

Jessica, the seventeen-year-old volunteer had also seen what happened and started to head over to pick everything up. Elena waved at her to stop.

"Shirley didn't have a very good night," Elena whispered to Jerry. "They've got her on some new drug. It seems to be helping a bit with her memory loss, but it's making her much more irritable. She's withdrawing more and more from our group activities."

"The doctor said they'd also increased the dosage of her high blood pressure pills," Jerry said.

"Yeah, they did. That's one of the side-effects of the new drug. They've got her on so many drugs now she could probably open her own pharmacy." Elena gave a heavy sigh. "I hope it's all worth it."

Jessica was pleading with her eyes for permission to help Shirley. When Shirley started to pick the puzzle pieces off the floor herself, Elena finally waved Jessica over to help.

"Should I help?" Jerry asked.

"Give her a few more minutes to compose herself," Elena said. "She's still learning how to deal with her frustrations. We don't want her to feel embarrassed about her little outburst."

Jerry waited another minute or two before heading over to Shirley. "We should probably get you a bigger table for your puzzles," he said as he approached.

Shirley's face flushed as she quickly picked the last few pieces up off the floor. "Oh, hello," she said as she straightened her hair. "Are you one of the new patients here?"

Jessica looked confused. "This is Jerry, one of our volunteers. He spoke to you just a couple of days ago."

"I don't think so," Shirley said. "We've got so few men around here, I'm sure I would have remembered him."

"Don't worry about it," Jerry said. "Jessica, why don't you go see if anyone else needs help? I'm going to help Shirley with this puzzle."

* * *

Cheech sat in the small meeting room of the advertising company, waiting for his interview to begin. He'd been surprised when he got the call to come in for a face-to-face meeting; he'd stumbled across their job posting online and only applied because he had no other prospects in the hopper.

He scanned the pictures on the wall showing posters of some of the successful marketing campaigns the company had developed. They all seemed to be for small companies claiming to have found the *next big thing*. There was also a picture of the founding partners of the firm, three men in their late twenties or early thirties. Not a good sign. Cheech noticed that their last names had the initials of N, B and T. Guess the company name didn't stand for "Next Big Thing" after all. Or maybe that's why they were the name partners. Cheech shuddered at the thought.

There was a soft knock on the door and an attractive brunette who looked to be in her late twenties entered. There was something about the way she carried herself that indicated she had some depth to her. Cheech rose to meet her.

"Hello," she said as she reached out her hand. "I'm Melanie Johnson, one of the managers here at NBT.

Cheech shook her hand. "Ian Martin, nice to meet you."

"Thanks for coming in to meet with me," she said as they sat down. She slid one of her business cards over to him and Cheech noticed that the title on the card said she was an advertising associate, not a manager.

For the first twenty minutes of the interview, they went through the standard questions and answers. Melanie described the type of work the firm engaged in, mostly marketing campaigns for small start-up companies hoping to make it big. Cheech described a few of the successful marketing campaigns he had run at his old car company. But Cheech had a sense that what *wasn't* being said was more important.

Melanie stopped taking notes and put down her pen. "Forgive me for saying this, but you're much older than I was expecting. You realize this position is a relatively junior position, right? You have so much experience. Why did you apply?"

"Because I need a job," Cheech said. "And when you're over fifty, finding a job, even a junior position, is damn near impossible."

Cheech figured he wasn't going to get the job anyway, so he decided to ask the question that had been lingering in the back of his mind. "But you knew I was over-qualified before I got here. Your clients are small start-ups and my experience is with a huge corporation. Why did you ask me to come in for an interview?"

She leaned back in her chair and studied him before answering. "Because of who you used to work for."

Cheech was confused.

Melanie leaned forward. "Talk on the street is that your old employer is not happy with their current advertising company and is open for pitches from new firms with fresh ideas. We're planning to bid on the business."

"Good luck with that," Cheech said. "Car companies don't work with small companies like yours, only the big firms."

"That's what the partners here said too, but I convinced them to let me create and lead a new auto group to go after the business."

"You have an auto group?"

Melanie's face flushed a little. "Well, technically I *am* the auto group right now, but I'm looking to add people, the right kind of people."

Cheech could see the passion in her. He remembered when he was young and full of piss and vinegar, before he'd taken so many body blows that had knocked the wind out of him. "You really think you can win the business?"

"I'm sure of it," Melanie said. "Will you help me?"

"I'm not sure how much help I'll be. If you haven't already heard, they fired me. Said I was too old."

Melanie looked directly at him. "Are you?"

Cheech looked straight back. "Hell, no!"

CHAPTER 13: CHRISTMAS PRESENTS

Elena supervised as Jessica, Emily and Jerry worked to maneuver all of the residents into the main hall at Shady Oaks. There was a buzz of excitement as they gathered to draw names for the Christmas gift exchange. Jessica, still a kid at heart, seemed the most excited of them all.

"Can I borrow your hat please?" Jessica asked one of the residents. Technically, Stanley wasn't supposed to wear a hat inside Shady Oaks, but no one had the heart to enforce the rule. He had first worn it a few years ago to cover up the scars and bandages from getting treatments for the melanoma that started appearing on his bald head, ironically caused by spending too much time outside in the sun without a hat. Since then, the hat had become part of his persona.

He gladly handed his hat to Jessica who started putting little pieces of paper into it, each containing the name of one of the residents. She shook the hat to shuffle up the names.

"Okay, Christmas is only three weeks away and this is for our Secret Santa gift exchange. Whoever's name you get, just get them a small present to open on Christmas day. It doesn't have to be big or expensive. I know many of you have been making things in our arts and crafts classes that would be perfect gifts." She scanned the people in the room. "Who wants to go first?"

Several hands shot up and Jessica headed over to the first person to raise their hand. "Janet, just reach in and pick a name."

Janet pulled out a piece of paper and opened it to read the name. "Oh good, I got Betty's name," she said.

"Shush," Jessica whispered. "Remember, it's supposed to be a secret."

Jessica moved through the room, allowing each of the seniors to select a name. Almost everyone announced the name they had selected, so there weren't going to be many secrets left to reveal come Christmas day. But that didn't matter. They all seemed to enjoy these types of activities.

Finally, Jessica headed over to Shirley who was sitting by herself at the back of the room. Shirley reached into the hat, pulled out the last remaining piece of paper and opened it to read the name.

"I don't know who that is," Shirley whispered.

Jessica didn't even look at the piece of paper because she already knew whose name was on it. "Oh, good for you," Jessica said. "You picked Jerry's name." She pointed to him. "You remember Jerry."

Elena rolled her eyes. Volunteers were not supposed to participate in the gift exchange. She knew that Jessica had rigged the draw to ensure that Shirley would draw Jerry's name.

"Jessica, could I have a word with you please?"

Jessica slowly walked toward her, her face taking on a crimson tone.

"I don't suppose you know how Jerry's name happened to end up in the hat, do you?" Elena said.

"I'm sorry. I guess I must have put it in there by mistake." Jessica hung her head, refusing to make eye contact. "It's just that Shirley doesn't want to participate in any of our group activities anymore. Jerry's the only one she ever talks to."

"Well, there's not much we can do about it now, is there?"

"Sorry. It'll never happen again."

Elena let the silence linger for a few seconds. "Dismissed," she finally said.

* * *

It was about a week before Christmas and Cheech was wandering aimlessly through the mall. He really didn't have much to buy, which was a good thing, because he'd now been out of work for several months and his bank account had been dropping at an alarming rate. He hadn't thought about money for most of his life, but it seemed to be becoming a point of stress for him now that he didn't have any coming in. He wished he hadn't pissed away so much of it on the sports car.

He'd already shipped presents to his parents out in Victoria. They'd invited him there for Christmas, but he'd declined, saying he was following up on some leads for a new job. That was a lie. He really only had one prospect, the junior position at NBT, and he wasn't sure that was going to come through either.

As he walked through the sports store, he came across a golf jacket that would be good for his wife. *Ex-wife? No, that wasn't right either. What do you call your ex when you're just separated, but not divorced? Jeez, I was so stupid. I can't believe I screwed that up.*

He looked at the tag on the jacket. It was waterproof, including zippers that would prevent the rain from leaking through. It had a waist and cuffs that you could cinch up tight so the jacket wouldn't flop around while you swung. He knew Maggie had been looking for one just like it for quite a while. *Are you supposed to buy a Christmas present for your wife when you're separated? Probably not, but that seems harsh. Send her a card? No, that doesn't seem right either.*

"Are you finding everything okay?" a sales clerk asked.

The question jolted Cheech back into reality. "Yeah, I'm just wondering whether this would be right for my wife."

"We just got it in," the clerk said. "It's next year's model. We don't normally bring in golf apparel until the spring, but we thought we'd bring in a few for Christmas this year. They've been selling quite well."

Cheech heard the musical tone of his cell phone and reached into his pocket. "Excuse me, I've got to take this call," he said to the clerk when he saw who was calling.

"No problem. Just let me know if you need anything."

Cheech swiped his phone to answer the call. "Hello, Ian Martin speaking."

"Hello, this is Melanie Johnson from NBT. Is this a good time to talk?"

Cheech moved back into the corner of the store away from the noise. "Sure, I'm just out doing some Christmas shopping. I've been hoping you'd call."

"Well, I've got some good news. We've been shortlisted by your old company to come in to present a marketing strategy to them. Presentation happens in early April, so we've only got three months to put it all together. The partners here have authorized me to offer you a three-month contract to help us flesh it out. If we win the business, we'll hire you on full time. I know you were hoping for a full-time position right away, but that's all they're prepared to offer right now. Still interested?"

"Absolutely," Cheech said.

"Wonderful. Are you available tomorrow around two to come in and work out the details?"

"Sure, that sounds good. Thanks so much."

Cheech felt the pressure release from his shoulders as he ended the call. He started to walk out of the store, but stopped again at the jackets. He searched through them until he found his wife's size, pulled it from the rack and headed for the checkout.

"Merry Christmas."

* * *

It was early afternoon on Christmas day and Max looked out the window at his father's place hoping his sister Karen would arrive soon. Although the tree was lit up and his father's place was decorated for Christmas, it had been eerily quiet all morning. Both Max and his father had been up for hours, but they were waiting for Karen to arrive before they exchanged presents.

Suddenly the door burst open and Karen came stumbling in carrying several packages. "Sorry I'm late. We had the usual Christmas chaos at our house this morning. Now that the kids are older, you'd think they wouldn't get as excited anymore at Christmas, but they still act like three-year-olds when they start to open presents."

Max wished he had been there to see it.

"Merry Christmas, Max," Karen said.

She kissed him on the cheek while still holding the packages. Then she quickly pulled them from the bags and placed them under the tree. She shuffled forward on her knees toward her father who was sitting in the same chair he always sat in and gave him a hug.

"Merry Christmas, Dad."

"Merry Christmas, dear," he replied.

Karen noticed an opened present sitting on the table beside her father. "Did you start opening presents without me?"

"No," Max said. "That's from Sylvia." Sylvia was the home care worker who helped take care of their father for a few hours every day during the week. "She gave Dad a book yesterday before she left on her Christmas break."

"It's large print," their father added. "She knows I don't see as well as I used to."

"That was sweet of her," Karen said.

"I made coffee," Max said. "You want some?"

"No, I'm already pretty wired." Karen took a quick glance at her watch. "Let's get started opening presents. I have to be back home in about an hour to put the turkey in."

They proceeded to open the presents lying under the tree. Karen had purchased several small items for both of them; she preferred that over big presents. Max had purchased expensive sweaters for both his sister and his father. He never knew what to get anyone and sweaters seemed to be his go-to present.

After the last package had been opened, Karen reached into her purse and pulled out an envelope. "This is for you," she said as she handed it to Max.

Max had no idea what could be inside. He slowly opened the envelope and pulled out the contents. "How did you…?"

"What is it?" their father asked.

"Tickets to the Masters," Karen said.

The Masters is a golf tournament held every year in

April in Augusta, Georgia. It's the first major tournament of the year, one of only four, and many consider it the toughest to win. Tickets to the tournament were almost impossible to get.

"I know you said you always wanted to go there," Karen said. "It's just for one of the practice rounds. That's all I could get. I entered a lottery for them and I won!"

Max's mouth hung open.

"Do you like them?" Karen asked.

"I'm overwhelmed," Max finally said.

Karen took a quick glance at her father and then locked eyes with Max.

"There's two tickets in there. I was hoping you'd take Dad with you."

* * *

Jerry arrived at Shady Oaks just as the Secret Santa gift exchange was getting underway. Everyone was dressed in their best outfits and there was a buzz of excitement in the room.

"I believe Shirley has a present for you," Jessica said when she saw him. She pointed to Shirley, who seemed to be hanging back from all of the festivities.

"Merry Christmas," Jerry said as he sat down beside her.

"Hello," Shirley said.

"Are you enjoying the party?"

She didn't answer, but looked at him with a confused expression.

Jerry saw the small package sitting on her lap. "Is that for me?"

Shirley looked at the package, but couldn't remember how it got there. She read the name on the label.

"Are you Jerry?"

"Yes, I am."

She handed him the package. When he opened it, he found it contained a key chain that had his name spelled out in small coloured stones that had been glued onto its leather tab. He remembered the arts and crafts class when they had all worked on them.

"It's lovely," Jerry said. "Thanks so much."

Jerry reached into his coat pocket. "Here, I got you a little something as well."

He handed her a small snow globe that had a classic-looking hotel inside, situated alongside a river. She shook the globe and watched as the snowflakes fell from the sky and landed on the hotel and the evergreen trees surrounding it.

"Thank you so much," Shirley said. "It looks so elegant. Did you travel there recently?"

"No, I haven't been there in quite a few years, but it's always been one of my favourite places. It's in Saskatchewan. I thought you might like it."

Shirley shook the snow globe again. "It looks so pretty and peaceful there. I think I'd like to go there sometime."

* * *

It was almost midnight that night as Elena made her last round of the day to check on all of her charges at Shady Oaks. It had been a busy day, but a great day. All of the family and visitors had returned to their own homes and the residents had been in bed for several hours.

As she passed by Shirley's room, she was surprised to see a lamp on. Shirley was sitting in her chair with the snow globe in her hand. Tears were streaming down her cheeks.

"Shirley, what's the matter?" Elena asked.

Shirley shook the globe and watched the snowflakes settle onto the castle-like hotel and the surrounding trees.

"I remember," she said.

CHAPTER 14: THE SOUTHERN SWING

Ray stood on the balcony of the condo in Cocoa Beach, Florida, watching the waves crash onto the shore. He loved the sound of the ocean and the warm, salty air. He and his wife, Candice, rented the condo every January and February and encouraged family and friends to visit them as often as they could.

"We should probably be heading to the airport," Candice shouted from the living room. "Amanda's flight should be arriving in just over an hour."

Their daughter and her family were flying into Orlando, about an hour's drive from Cocoa Beach.

Ray slid the balcony door closed and was pulling his car keys out of his pocket when the phone rang. He was surprised to hear Amanda's voice when he answered.

"Was your flight early?" he asked.

"No, Dad. We're still in Toronto. I'm sorry, but we're not coming."

"Why? What happened?"

"They kicked us off the plane. Tyler threw one of his tantrums just before we took off and we couldn't get him to calm down. They said he was jeopardizing the safety of the other passengers, so they made us get off."

"Is he okay?"

"Yeah, he's fine – now. He's just sitting here calm as can be. The airline offered to put us on a later flight if he remained like he is now, but Doug said he doesn't want to chance it, so they're just going to refund us the price of the tickets."

"Are you sure that's what you want to do? The weather down here is supposed to be hot and sunny all week. Perfect beach weather. I know how much you like the beach."

"We do, especially Tyler, but I'm not sure we can fly with him anymore. Now that he's bigger, he's harder to control. He punched me when I tried to get him to calm down. Wouldn't surprise me if I end up with a black eye."

Ray desperately tried to think of a solution, but he had nothing to offer. Candice motioned for him to hand her the phone and Ray watched as Amanda explained the whole thing again to her mother. Candice sighed when she hung up the phone.

"Isn't there something you can do?" she asked Ray.

"Like what?"

"I don't know. I was *so* looking forward to this week with them. What are we going to do now?"

Good question. Ray headed out onto the balcony to think. They had crammed the week with activities to do with the kids. Now they were faced with spending the whole time with just the two of them, without anyone or anything else to act as a distraction or a buffer.

He looked over his shoulder and saw his wife sitting on the couch with her eyes shut. She sure spent a lot of time sleeping these days. *Was she tired? Was she tired of him?*

He moved off the balcony and back into the living room. "Do you feel like going for a walk on the beach?"

Candice opened her eyes. "With you?"

"Yes, with me. Got anything better to do?"

Candice looked at him, appearing somewhat confused. "Sure, let me grab a hat."

They took the elevator down to the lobby in silence and then walked along the short path that lead down to the beach.

"Which way do you want to head?" Ray asked.

Candice looked left and right. She could see some storm clouds forming in the south. "Let's head north," she said.

They walked along the beach for several minutes without saying a word to each other. Periodically, Candice would stop to examine a sea shell that had washed up on shore.

Ray found a pure white angel-wing shell that he knew Candice would love and handed it to her. "Have I told you lately that I love you?"

She looked at him, squinting her eyes in the bright sunlight. "No. I can't remember the last time you said it."

"I do. I guess I should tell you more often."

They continued to walk along the beach. "This is where you're supposed to say you love me too," Ray said.

"You think I don't?"

"It would be nice to hear it every once in a while."

She reached out and took his hand. "Yes, I still love you."

They continued to walk along the beach.

"Are you happy?" Ray asked.

"I suppose," Candice said. "I'm just worried about

Amanda and the kids. I'm disappointed they're not coming to visit. I had so much planned. The beach, mini-golf, Disney World. I was looking forward to doing all of it with them."

"We still can, you know," Ray said.

"Just the two of us? Don't be silly. Disney World is for kids. We're too old to go without the kids."

"Come on. It'll be fun. They say it's for *kids of all ages.*"

Candice poked him in the ribs. "You just read that in the brochure."

"Absolutely, but I still think it'll be fun. Let's do everything we were going to do next week with the kids, but just the two of us."

* * *

Bruce and Marilyn also headed south for a few months every winter, although they preferred the area around Clearwater on the west coast of Florida. Every year, they invited their kids down to stay with them for a week's vacation. Emma and Paige had come down in previous years during March break, but they wouldn't be coming this year because they said they couldn't afford it.

"I wish the girls were coming down again this winter," Marilyn said.

"Yeah, I do too," Bruce said, "but they've got to start paying their own way. They're adults now. Josh has always paid his own way."

"Yeah, but he's working."

"So is Paige, and Emma's working part-time. They've got to realize the *Bank of Mom and Dad* is now closed."

Marilyn sighed. She agreed with her husband, but she still didn't like it. "What time does Josh's flight get in?"

"Just after lunch, but he's renting a car so we don't

have to pick him up."

Josh planned to be in Florida for a week, but would only be spending a day or two with them. He and some friends were staying in a hotel in Tampa and had numerous activities scheduled, including some deep-sea fishing. Bruce convinced him to fit in a round of golf with them mid-week and Josh said he'd be bringing one of his friends to make it a foursome.

They lucked out on the weather and Bruce and Marilyn were sitting in their golf cart on the first tee waiting for Josh and his friend to arrive. Josh had called to say they were running a little late, but he thought they'd still get there before their tee time. Bruce grumbled and checked his watch, again.

"There he is," Marilyn said.

They were both surprised when they saw the friend.

"Did you know he was bringing a girl?" Marilyn asked.

"No," Bruce said. "He just said he'd be bringing a friend."

They came racing up in a golf cart a few minutes later.

"Hi, Mom and Dad," Josh said as he bounced out of the cart. "This is Robyn. Robyn, this is my father, Bruce, and my mother, Marilyn."

Robyn was tall and thin and looked to be in her mid-twenties. She had striking red hair and her face also took on a reddish tinge as she came over to them. "Nice to meet you. Sorry we're late. It's my fault. I couldn't decide which outfit to wear."

"Well, you obviously chose the right one," Marilyn said.

That was an understatement. Robyn's outfit was coordinated right down to her socks and golf shoes.

"Dad, why don't you go ahead and tee off," Josh said. "I want to take a few practice swings."

Bruce teed off and hit a good shot. Josh hit next and easily out-drove his father by twenty yards, even without a proper warmup. Then they pulled their golf carts up to the ladies tee. Marilyn also hit a good shot and the focus turned to Robyn. She took a few practice swings which made it apparent that she was a pretty good golfer. But her nerves got the best of her and she barely hit her tee shot twenty yards.

"We'll give you a mulligan on that one," Bruce said. "You never really had time to warm up."

Robyn's face got even redder. "No, I just want to get off the first tee. I'll play that one."

Josh tried to reassure her as she got into the cart. She hit an iron on her second shot which sailed well down the fairway.

"That's more like it," she sighed in relief.

As they played the front nine, it became apparent to Bruce and Marilyn that Robyn was more than just a friend to their son. Every time they would ask Robyn a question, Josh hovered close by, ready to come to her rescue.

When they reached the tenth tee, Marilyn suggested they move the bags around on the carts so that Marilyn and Robyn could ride together. "This will give Robyn and I a chance to get to know each other a little better."

It was hard to object because the men's tee was back up on a ridge overlooking a small pond and the women's tee was down below on the other side of the pond. Josh shrugged his shoulders and mouthed "sorry" toward Robyn.

Bruce and Josh drove their cart to the top of the ridge. They had to wait on the tee as the group in front of them was still within range.

"So how long have you and Robyn been going out?"

Bruce asked.

"We're just friends, Dad."

Josh got out of the cart, walked to the front of the tee and peered down the hill where the ladies were waiting. Bruce grabbed his driver from his bag and walked up to stand beside him.

"Do you think Mom is grilling her with questions?" Josh asked.

"You know your mother. I can pretty much guarantee it."

Josh sighed. "We've only been going out a few months. When I told her I was coming down to Florida for a week with the guys, she decided to come down at the same time with one of her girlfriends. I like her, a lot, but we're not serious yet. I hope Mom doesn't wreck it for me."

Suddenly they both heard Robyn and Marilyn burst into laughter. The sound easily carried to the top of the ridge.

"What do you think they're laughing about?" Josh asked. "Is that a good sign?"

Bruce put his hand on his son's shoulder. "You'll find out soon enough." He pointed down the fairway. "It's your shot."

Josh teed his ball, but his mind was on anything but the shot. He hit the ground about three inches behind the ball and it fluttered off the top of the ridge and into the middle of the pond below. He reached into his pocket for another ball.

"There's a drop zone down below," Bruce said. "You can play your next shot from there."

Bruce hit his tee shot right down the middle. Then they got into their golf cart and drove slowly down the path. By the time they got to the bottom of the hill, both ladies had already teed off.

"The drop zone is over there," Bruce said. He pointed to a white circle that was just to the right of the ladies tee.

Robyn gave Josh a sly smile as he headed over to the drop zone. "Sorry you hit it in the water – *Pookie*."

Josh turned beet red and turned to look at his mother. She had called him *Pookie* when he was a baby, but she had promised not to call him that once he started school.

"Sorry," his mother said. "It just slipped out."

Robyn started to giggle, which prompted Marilyn to start to laugh and before they knew it, they were both roaring.

"Leave him alone and let him hit his shot," Bruce said.

Josh played terribly on the back nine, losing to his father by ten shots. He'd still never beaten his father in a head-to-head match. Though Bruce usually relished the competition, he took pity on him this day.

"I know you were a little off your game today worrying about Robyn and your mother, but I think you need some help with your putting." Josh had missed several three-footers during their round. "We've got a guy at our club that specializes in putting."

"I don't know, Dad. I was just off today."

"To me, it looks like your tempo is all off. There's nothing more important in putting than tempo." He wasn't sure Josh was listening. "You've got a birthday coming up in a few months. How about I get you a putting lesson for your present."

"I suppose. If you think it will help."

"Well, I don't think you'll ever beat me unless you improve your putting." Bruce knew that last dig would convince him.

"Sign me up," Josh said.

CHAPTER 15: AMEN CORNER

Max and his father, Arthur, slowly inched forward in their car as they approached the Augusta National Golf Club, site of the Masters. It had taken Max a couple of days to drive down from Canada because his father didn't like to fly anymore. Max had been worried about his father's health before the trip began, but he'd actually been doing pretty well so far. Arthur had constantly nagged him about his driving habits – you're driving too fast – you're driving too slow – you're in the wrong lane – so Max breathed a sigh of relief each day when his father drifted off to sleep. It allowed Max to drive in peace and much faster than he normally would.

"We'll never find a place to park," Arthur said.

"We'll be fine," Max said. Max could see the line of cars in front of him was over half a mile long. Although they were moving slowly, he was encouraged by the number of policemen directing traffic. "They do this every year. I'm sure they've got it down to a science by now."

Sure enough, once they turned onto the property,

there were volunteers stationed about every twenty yards or so, each directing the fans to exactly where they should park. Max was surprised that parking was free.

It was barely after seven on Wednesday morning and they had lucked out on the weather. Although it was a little cool right now, it was supposed to be sunny all day with the temperature rising to the high seventies in the afternoon.

The main tournament didn't start until Thursday, but all of the golfers were out this morning for their last practice round. As Max and his father walked from the parking lot through the main gates, they could see the practice range was already full of players.

"Do you think Tiger will be out this morning?" Arthur asked.

"I've heard he's going off in one of the first groups," Max said. "That's him warming up on the far right."

Although they were still over two hundred yards from the golfers and couldn't see their faces clearly, Max could identify each of the golfers just by their swings. It was amazing to see how distinctive each one was.

"That's Mark O'Meara beside him. I think they're playing together this morning." Max checked the tee sheet they'd been handed when they came through the gate. "Yes, they're teeing off in just a few minutes, along with Jim Furyk."

Max wanted to hurry along to see them tee off, but his father's pace was already starting to slow, even though they'd hardly covered any distance at all. They arrived at the practice tee just as Tiger finished his warmup. As he headed off to the first tee, several hundred people followed. Max knew his father would never be able to keep up with the horde of people following Tiger.

"Do you want me to see if they have any wheelchairs

available?" Max asked.

His father scowled. "I'm not a cripple. Don't need a goddam wheelchair!"

Max sighed because he knew his father would not be able to walk the course. "How about we just find a place to camp out and watch each of the golfers as they go by?"

Arthur nodded his agreement.

"Any particular hole you want to see?" Max asked.

"Amen Corner."

"Perfect." It was a part of the course that was also on Max's bucket list to see in person.

Amen Corner consisted of the second shot on the par four 11th hole, the par three 12th hole, and the first two shots on the par five 13th hole. The tricky winds in that corner of the golf course had destroyed the dreams of many a golfer hoping to win the Masters.

It took them almost an hour for Max and his father to walk to Amen Corner, as Arthur had to stop several times to rest. Max wished he had purchased one of the green Masters chairs. When they reached the 12th tee, Max looked for a place on the grass for them to sit, but his father headed directly over to one of the chairs already set up.

"I think those chairs are reserved," Max said, but his father ignored him.

It was common practice for patrons to place their chairs in some of the most popular spots on the course, staking out their claim to the spot even though they might not sit there the entire time. Arthur just plopped himself down in the first seat he saw. The lady in the next seat looked like she was about to tell them the seats were already taken, but held her tongue when she saw the sweat beading on his forehead.

She smiled at Max. "It's okay," she said in a southern

drawl. "The people sittin' there won't be back for a while. I don't think they'll mind you usin' 'em til they get back."

Max returned the smile. "Dad, you rest here for a bit. I'm going to get you a drink."

Max headed off to the concession stand. He bought two bottles of water and two pimento cheese sandwiches, handed the girl a ten-dollar bill and was surprised to get change back. At most big events, customers get gouged at the concession stands, but the Masters prided itself on charging low prices for food and drink. After all, the fans were their guests and they were treated like royalty.

When he got back to the 12th tee, the lady sitting beside Max invited him to sit down. The patrons who owned the chairs still hadn't returned to reclaim their seats. Max handed the water and sandwich to his father and encouraged him to drink. He hoped the long walk wouldn't prove to be too much for him.

Max looked at the pinks, purples and fuchsias of the azaleas and the white dogwoods that surrounded the warm greens of the golf course. He didn't see a weed anywhere and assumed they just died of embarrassment on such a beautiful property. Whenever the wind blew, the pollen from the trees and flowers hovered in the air before slowly settling, as if placing a protective blanket over everything. Although he was glued to the TV every year to watch the Masters and thought he knew everything about the golf course, Max found it was much hillier than he expected.

Max noticed the fans all look to the left to see the golfers approaching the 11th green and recognized the familiar profile of Mike Weir, the winner of the 2003 Masters. Mike was the first left-hander and only Canadian to ever win the Masters. Since then, a combination of injuries and poor play had dropped him well down the world rankings, but he was still invited back every year as a former champion. When he hit his second shot, the crowd followed the flight of the ball and saw it land short and bounce up onto the right fringe of the green.

"Missed the green," Arthur said. "He's not as good as he used to be. Maybe he should give up the tour and just go and be a club pro somewhere."

Max encouraged him to lower his voice and ignored the shot against club pros. "He's okay there. It's a pretty easy up-and-down from the fringe."

Max checked his tee sheet and saw that Weir was playing with Graham DeLaet and David Hearn, two up and coming Canadians. They had both out-driven Weir by thirty yards. Hearn hit first and they saw his approach shot land on the left side of the green. The crowd started to applaud, but then groaned as they watched the ball circle to the left and trickle down the bank into the pond. DeLaet hit next. His approach was just a little long and right, but the slope carried it even further to the right so he ended up almost twenty yards from the green in a valley, leaving a very difficult pitch shot. When they walked off the 11th green, Weir had made par and both DeLaet and Hearn had made bogies. It takes a lot of years of experience to learn how to play the 11th hole and sometimes the conservative play is the right play. Par is always a good score on that hole.

The crowd applauded as all three golfers walked the short distance from the 11th green to the 12th tee. They were now only about thirty feet from where Max and his father were sitting. They watched as Weir threw up some grass and watched the wind carry it. Then he pointed to the tops of the trees and the flags on the 11th and 12th greens.

"What's he doing?" Arthur asked. "Why doesn't he just hit the damn ball?"

Arthur didn't realize his voice was carrying farther than he expected. Max noticed several fans look at them with raised eyebrows and encouraged his father to lower his voice.

"He's teaching them about the wind on this hole," Max whispered.

One thing that was great to see was how the veterans of golf were willing to pass on the knowledge they had gained over the years. The 12th hole was only 155 yards long and would normally be a relatively easy shot for world-class pros. But the winds in Amen Corner made it one of the most treacherous shots in golf. If you were short or right, your ball would end up in Rae's Creek. If you were long, it was easy to make bogey or worse from the bunker or pine needles behind the green. Some golfers based their club selection on what the wind was doing at the top of the trees rather than down at ground level. Others would look at the flags on the 11th and 12th holes and base their shot selection on that.

Max noticed that the flag on the 11th green was blowing in the opposite direction as the one on the 12th, even though they were only about a hundred yards apart. Weir stood on the tee watching and waiting. Suddenly, the wind shifted and both flags were blowing in the same direction. Weir quickly stepped up to the ball, hit his shot onto the middle of the green and then gave out a deep sigh of relief.

"You know, if you'd worked a little harder, that could be you out there playing in the Masters," Arthur whispered to him.

Here we go. Max knew it was just a matter of time until

his father reminded him of his shortcomings.

"I'm not good enough, Dad."

"Not now, but when you were younger, you could have made it."

Max thought back to his younger days. He was good, very good. But he still remembered the day he realized he was not a tour caliber player. No one had to tell him, he just knew it in his bones. That was the day he decided to take a job as a club pro, start paying off some of his accumulated debt, and get on with his life. He still thought he had made the right decision. Back in the early days, it was tough to make a living playing golf. Now, the winner of a single PGA tournament can win almost as much as a legend like Arnold Palmer won in his whole career.

"No I couldn't, Dad. Even when I was younger, I just wasn't good enough. I'm happy being a club pro."

"Selling golf clubs and balls? You're just a glorified golf shirt salesman."

Max could feel his anger rising, but this wasn't the time or place to have this argument.

"I'm going to follow these guys down the next hole," Max said as he got out of his chair. "I'll be back in about half an hour."

Max followed the Canadians as they played the par-five 13th hole. Both DeLaet and Hearn hit the green in two shots and made easy birdies. Weir laid up on his second shot, but hit a good third onto the green and also made birdie.

Max thought about following them for a few more holes, but realized he should probably head back to check on his father. When he arrived back at the 12th tee, he saw the people who owned the seats had returned, but there was no sign of his father. He scanned the crowd, but didn't see him anywhere.

The lady who had been sitting beside him, waved to catch Max's attention. "I told him to wait 'til you got back, but he said he wanted to head over to find a good spot to watch the par-3 contest."

"Do you know which way he went?" Max asked.

The lady turned and pointed back up the hill. "Sorry, but he seemed pretty sure he could find it on his own."

Max knew there was nothing this lady could have done to stop him once his father made up his mind. *I shouldn't have left him.* Max climbed the hill behind the 12th tee. Given how slow his father walked, he couldn't have gone far.

The par-3 contest was held on probably the world's most beautiful nine hole course, located just north of the tenth hole of the main course. Most of the top players played in it because the main course was closed on Wednesday afternoon to allow the staff time to prepare the fairways and greens for tournament play beginning the next day.

Max walked quickly back along the 10th fairway, hoping he would soon catch up to his father, but there was no sign of him. There was no way he could have made it any further than that, so Max started to re-trace his path. Maybe he had walked back along the 18th fairway instead of the 10th. Max quickly walked along that hole, but there was no sign of his father there either.

Suddenly Max saw a small group of people behind the 17th green, all huddling around a man who was lying on the ground. *Oh, my God!!!* Max was sure it was his father and he raced over. He got there just in time to hear his father cursing a blue streak at the two paramedics who were trying to help him.

"Dad, are you okay?"

"I just lost my balance, that's all," his father yelled. "I'm fine."

"I'm sure you are," one of the paramedics said. "But we have to take you into the medical centre just to make sure." She smiled at Arthur. "You wouldn't want me to lose my job, would you?"

Max could see that she was using all of her charms to try to get his father to cooperate.

"I suppose not," Arthur said.

The two paramedics helped him into the back of a specially designed golf cart. They signaled for Max to ride up in the front seat. When they got him to the medical centre, they put electrodes on Arthur's chest to do an electrocardiogram, but everything looked okay.

"Can we go now?" he asked. "We want to watch the par-3 contest."

The female paramedic looked at Max. "Is he always this crusty?" she whispered.

"Always," Max said. "Welcome to my world."

"Well, he taught us all a few more curse words today."

She pasted on a fake smile and turned to his father. "Maybe it's best if you just stay here with us for a bit longer." She helped him into a wheelchair and then pushed him into a very small adjoining room that had a television hanging in the corner. "I think they're showing the par-3 contest on TV."

* * *

The next day, Arthur slept almost the entire way while Max started the drive north to Canada. They were just on the outskirts of Lexington, Kentucky, when Max started getting tired and decided to look for a hotel. Because his father had slept in the car for most of the day, he wasn't tired at all. After they grabbed something to eat, they turned on the TV in their room to watch the highlights of the first round of the tournament.

"I'm sorry I messed up our day at the Masters," Arthur said.

"It wasn't your fault. We probably tried to do too much walking."

"I used to be able to walk for miles," Arthur said. "Now I can't seem to do anything by myself. I hate always having someone around to take care of me."

"Don't worry about it, Dad. You're eighty-six. Don't be afraid to ask for help if you need it."

They both turned to watch the TV. Eventually, Max's eyes started to close.

"I wanted to prove to you that I could still do some things on my own," Arthur said. "But I couldn't."

Max heard the crack in his father's voice and opened his eyes.

"I got turned all around and couldn't figure out which way to go," Arthur continued. "And then I started feeling dizzy and sick. I started calling for your mother, which is stupid, because I know she's dead, but I needed help and I didn't know where you were." He was trying not to cry. "I thought I was going to die."

Max saw the tears welling up in his father's eyes and hurried over to hug him. "I'm sorry Dad. I shouldn't have left you alone. The paramedics said you're fine. You're *not* going to die." Max smiled at him. "You're probably going to out-live us all."

* * *

The next morning they were up early to continue their drive back to Canada. Max had heard his father get up several times during the night to go to the bathroom. Since he had hardly slept overnight, Arthur fell asleep shortly after they started driving again. It was funny. On the trip down, Max was glad when his father fell asleep so he wasn't constantly nagging him about his driving. But this time, he missed it.

They were just outside of Toledo, Ohio, when Max noticed the sweat on his father's face and forehead. He gently pushed on his father's shoulder to wake him up.

"Dad, are you okay?"

Arthur opened his eyes and looked at him. The look on his face told him that he wasn't. He grabbed his chest. "I – can't – breathe," he gasped.

Max knew he had to find a hospital and fortunately, the road sign showed there was one at the next exit. He took it and then raced through a few intersections trying to figure out which way to go. When he saw a sign indicating the hospital was left at the next corner, he crossed several lanes of traffic to make the turn, ignoring the blaring horns and screeching brakes of the cars he cut off. He drove up to the emergency doors and leapt out of the driver's seat.

"Help! My father's having a heart attack!!!"

A couple of nurses who were leaving the hospital after their shift immediately came over to help. Within seconds, Arthur was on a stretcher and wheeled into emergency.

Max paced back and forth in the waiting room. *Was this going to be how it ended?* Although his relationship with his father had been strained for decades and his health had been getting worse over the last few years, Max still felt woefully unprepared. He thought he was going to throw up.

A middle-aged nurse came into the waiting room. "Are you the son of Mr. Wakelam?"

"Yes," Max replied. "How's he doing? Did he have a

heart attack?"

"He's stable. His heart is fine, but he seems to be having trouble breathing. We'd like to run some tests. Do you have insurance?"

Max remembered that his sister had taken out a medical insurance policy for him just a few weeks before they started their vacation. He hadn't thought it was necessary because they were only going to be out of Canada for a few days, but Karen had insisted. He was now glad she had.

"Yes, we took out insurance for him before we left Canada." Max tried to remember what he'd done with the paperwork that Karen had given him. "I think I've got the policy somewhere in my luggage. Do you need it now?"

The nurse seemed relieved. "No, we'll go ahead with the tests as long as you're sure you're covered. It'll take several hours to run these tests and we'll probably keep your father overnight. While you're waiting, I'd suggest you find the policy and provide the details to our administrator, up on the second floor." She reached out to touch Max's arm. "We'll take good care of your father."

Max thanked her and then headed out to his car. He had left it parked in a drop-off zone outside of the emergency department. It was only then that he realized he hadn't even locked the car.

"I was hoping you'd be back," an elderly gentleman in a black security uniform said. "You're not allowed to park there, but I've been keeping an eye on it for you while you were inside."

"Thanks," Max said. "I wasn't thinking very clearly when I arrived."

"I figured as much. There's a parking lot just back up

the laneway on your right. I'd suggest getting a day-pass if you think you're going to be here for a while."

Max drove to the parking lot and then searched through his luggage for the insurance policy. He couldn't find it, so he decided to call his sister. He should probably call her and tell her the situation anyway.

"The policy is in the left outside pocket of Dad's suitcase," Karen told him.

Then she grilled Max with a barrage of questions, very few of which he could answer. At this point, Max didn't have much information to give her, but he promised he'd call again as soon as he did.

He headed back inside the hospital looking for the administration department. When he got there, a young clerk just took down the name of the insurance company and the policy number. She didn't even look at the actual policy.

It was just after midnight when the nurse came into the waiting room to find Max. She tapped him on the shoulder to get his attention, as he had nodded off while waiting.

"We have the results of your father's tests," she said. "It turns out he's got a chest infection, but he's going to be fine. It appears that it was triggered by an allergic reaction to pollen. He said he first started having trouble breathing while you were in Georgia."

"Yeah, my dad had some problems when we were at the Masters, but I thought that was because he'd just done too much walking."

Max remembered the yellow and green pollen he'd seen falling from the trees whenever the wind blew in Augusta.

"We've got him on oxygen right now and he's resting comfortably. I think he'll be good to go first thing in the morning."

* * *

The following morning, Max held his father's arm as they walked from the emergency department out to the car. He seemed to be breathing quite comfortably now.

Max navigated out of the parking lot and began looking for signs telling him how to get back on the freeway.

"You're in the wrong lane," his father said.

Max smiled at him. "It's good to have you back, Dad."

CHAPTER 16: TEMPO & TIMING

In the spring, every golfer looks forward to the upcoming season, confident that this is going to be the year their game finally comes together. Josh was going to take advantage of the putting lesson his father got him for his birthday and pulled into the parking lot at the Riverview Golf Club. He noticed the license plate of the car he parked beside read "OnePutt".

"I'm here for a putting lesson with Grant," Josh said as he approached the counter inside the pro shop.

"I think G is still out on the range giving another lesson," Scott said. "He should be back any sec."

Sure enough, Grant came into the pro shop a few minutes later. He invited Josh to the small indoor putting green they had set up in the back of the pro shop. Grant had set up the monitors before he arrived, so all he had to do was attach a small device to the shaft of Josh's putter. He told Josh to hit about six or seven putts toward the hole which was about ten feet away.

"Okay, that should be enough," Grant said. "Let's see what the monitor says." Grant clicked a button on his computer and a bunch of charts and graphs appeared. "Your putting stroke is actually quite good. Your putter is pretty much in alignment to the target at address. Your swing path is slightly to the inside and the putter face is a bit closed at impact, but only by fractions. Your tempo seems good and your launch angle is about two degrees. Everything looks good. What made you think you need help with your putting?"

"I miss a ton of three and four-footers," Josh said.

Grant clicked a button on his mouse and another chart appeared. "According to this, if you're reading the putts correctly, you should be making between ninety-two and ninety-six percent of three foot putts."

"I wish that was true," Josh said. "I doubt I make half of them."

Grant reached down and removed the device from the shaft of Josh's putter. "Why don't we head outside and see how you do on a real putting green?"

When they got outside, Grant made a small adjustment to Josh's grip and then watched him hit several ten-foot putts. Everything looked good.

Then he placed several balls in a circle about four feet from the hole. Josh made the first two which were uphill putts, but lipped out on the next two and then missed the hole entirely on the last two attempts. It was like an entirely different person was now holding the putter.

"Why are you hitting your putts so hard?" Grant asked.

"I read an article in a golf magazine that said the pro's on the tour hit their short putts firm and try to take the break out."

Grant knew this was partly true, but it wasn't good advice for a typical amateur. "I think you'd be better to hit the ball in at the *proper* pace, rather than trying to ram it into the back of the cup. It's causing you to jab down on the ball which is causing the ball to bounce off the putter face. It's also throwing off your tempo. Golf is all about tempo and timing."

Josh remembered his father saying the same thing.

Grant placed the balls again in a four-foot circle around the hole. "This time, try to hit the putts so they only go about six to twelve inches past the hole if you miss."

Josh tried again and this time made four out of six attempts. The ones he missed were the downhill putts, one which was straight downhill and the other had a left-to-right break.

"Okay, your speed was much better on those putts, but you decelerated on your downhill putts, which is causing you to leave the putter face open at impact. That's why you missed both of those putts to the right."

"I guess I was afraid of hitting the downhill putts too hard," Josh said. "If I miss, I don't want to have another three-footer coming back."

"Downhill putts with a left-to-right break are the hardest, even for the pros, and they putt on really fast greens. On the tour, who do you think has the best tempo?"

Josh thought for a second. "Probably, Ernie Els."

"Perfect," Grant said. "In golf, your backswing should take about twice as long as your through stroke. So what I want you to do is say his name when you putt. Say *Ern-ie* when you take the putter back and *Els* on your forward stroke."

Josh tried it again and this time made all six of the putts. "Geez, I wish I could putt like this when I'm out on the course."

Grant smiled. "Most people putt like pros on the

practice green. The problem is, there's more pressure during the actual round. So, let's create a drill to try to create some of that pressure while practicing." Grant placed the balls in a circle around the hole again. "I want to see you make twelve in a row."

Josh easily made the first six. He made the seventh and eighth putts as well, but they just curled in the side of the hole. His ninth putt lipped out.

"Okay, start over," Grant said.

Josh tried again. The next time he didn't miss until the tenth putt.

"Start over," Grant said.

This time Josh made eleven in a row. He took a deep breath before he attempted to make the last one. He left the last putt six inches short. "Shit, shit, shit!!! How can I leave a four foot putt six inches short?"

Grant laughed. "It's because the pressure caused you to lose your tempo. Try it again and this time say *Ern-ie Els* out loud when you make the stroke."

Josh did and the putt rolled into the centre of the cup.

"But I can't say his name out loud every time I putt. People will think I'm crazy."

"You're probably right. So just say it inside your head. When you're out on the course and you start missing short putts, start thinking about this little drill to get your tempo back. Or if you're on the last hole and you need to sink a four-footer to win the club championship, you know the pressure is going to get to you. So just imagine yourself on the practice green, say *Ern-ie Els* to yourself when you make the stroke, and you'll find the centre of the cup."

After the lesson was over, Josh continued to practice his putting for another half an hour. He was sure he'd beat his father in their next match.

* * *

Cheech came into the small boardroom at NBT. Melanie's auto group now consisted of four people, including Cheech and herself. They had already held several brainstorming sessions to come up with a new advertising strategy. Each person had tweaked their favourite idea, but today was the day they were hoping to make the final decision on which one to present to the client.

Cheech was at least twenty-five years older than anyone else in the group and he knew the two new hires wondered why an old fart like him was part of their team.

Brent pitched his idea of emphasizing the car's sound system in their advertising. "Kids today like to listen to their favourite tunes when they're in their car. We've got a great speaker system including two speakers in the back. In addition to the radio and CD player, the system allows them to plug in their iPod or MP3 player so they can listen to their whole collection while they're driving." He placed a series of four storyboard pictures on the table showing four young people driving out to the beach.

"Looks like they're partying," Cheech said.

"Exactly," Brent said. "In order to attract the young driver to the car, I think we should show all of the fun they could have if they had a car like this."

Melanie studied the pictures. "Looks good."

Then she turned to Ashley. She was a brand new hire, fresh out of school. "What's your idea?"

"I like Brent's idea, but I also think we should heavily advertise the phone integration. Kids live on their phones today and they always want to be connected, so I think we should emphasize that in our advertising." Her storyboard pictures showed the vehicle's ability to connect to the internet.

"Remember, we're trying to sell a car, not a new phone or computer," Cheech said.

"You don't like these ideas?" Melanie asked.

"No, they're good ideas and those are important features to include in our advertising, but I think they have to be targeted at the ultimate decision maker."

"They are," Ashley protested. "The target market for this vehicle is the first-time buyer looking for something fun to drive."

"Yeah, it's not targeted at someone like you," Brent added. "You wouldn't be caught dead in a trendy car like this. No offence, but I think it's targeted at someone much younger."

Cheech smiled. "No offence taken. You're right. I'm not the one going to be driving around in a car like this. It's for people like yourselves."

"Precisely," Ashley said. "In fact, I've been thinking of buying one myself."

Cheech turned to her. "Good, so let's use your situation as a sample case study. What features attracted you to this vehicle?"

Ashley listed all of the features they'd already discussed, plus the fact that it came in a bright canary-yellow colour that she just adored.

"So why haven't you bought it yet?"

Ashley looked away. "My dad wants me to buy a Corolla. He said his first vehicle was a Corolla."

Cheech could not hide his grin. "Your dad? If it's going to be your vehicle, why does it matter what your dad thinks?"

Ashley's face flushed. "Because he said he'd help pay for it if I got a Corolla. I'm still paying off my student loans, so I can't afford it on my own."

It was almost as if Cheech knew what she was going to say. "So, we actually have two decision makers in this purchase, you and your father."

"I guess," Ashley admitted.

"I think I see your point," Melanie said, "but I'm not sure how this affects our marketing strategy. We can't target two completely different customers in our advertising."

"Actually, I think we can," Cheech said. "We still show how the vehicle can connect to the internet, but instead of showing how the kid can find the location of the pub they're looking for, show how it can be used to find another route home when the main road is blocked off. Instead of showing how she can call all her friends on the phone while driving, show how she can call her father to come rescue her when she gets stuck in a snowbank."

Ashley's eyes lit up. "If I could convince my father that I'd actually be safer with all of these features, then I think he'd let me buy it instead of the Corolla."

"When a kid buys his or her first car, they almost always ask their parents for advice," Cheech said. "The kids want something cool. The parents want something safe. So any advertising has to be delivering messages to both at the same time."

"It sounds like we have a plan," Melanie said. "Let's work out the details. The pitch to the client is only a few weeks away."

* * *

It was a couple of weeks later when Melanie came over to Cheech's cubicle at the office.

"Well, I think we're ready for tomorrow's meeting with the client. The partners are coming to do the corporate portion and I'll be doing the presentation on our marketing strategy. I was wondering if you'd like to come and do it with me?"

"I'm not sure that's a good idea," Cheech said.

"But a lot of these ideas are yours. We couldn't have done it without your help."

"Thanks. I appreciate you saying that, but they're looking for someone young with fresh, new ideas. I think the presence of an old guy like me would actually hurt your chances of winning the business."

"You really think so?"

"I know so." Cheech knew that most of these new ideas were actually the same ones that he wanted to pitch to his boss when he still worked there – the ones they never even bothered to listen to before showing him out the door.

Cheech looked at the confident young woman standing in front of him, almost like she was his daughter. "I think you're exactly the type of person they're looking for right now. The timing is perfect."

CHAPTER 17: MONEY GAMES

Ray headed into the local branch of his bank and approached the young, twenty-something girl at the front desk.

"I'd like to talk to one of your advisors about my RRSP," he said.

"Are you here to make a contribution?" she asked. "I can probably help you with that."

"No, I'd actually like to take some money out."

The girl looked at him as if he had suddenly pulled out a weapon. "Take money out? Are you sure?" She looked completely perplexed. "I'm not sure I know how to do that."

One of the advisors happened to be coming out of his office at the time and she waved him over. "This man wants to take money *out* of his RRSP," she whispered to the advisor. They both looked at Ray with puzzled looks on their faces. Finally, the advisor spoke.

"I'm Jim Waters," he said. "Why don't you come into my office, Mister...?"

"Ferguson, Ray Ferguson."

Ray followed him into his office and the advisor closed the door behind them.

"Are you unhappy with our service, sir?"

"No, the service has been fine. I've been banking here for almost fifteen years, regularly putting money into my RRSP. I'd now like to take some of it out."

The advisor still didn't seem to understand.

"We spent a little more than we expected in Florida this year," Ray explained, "so I'm running a bit short on cash."

"Would you like to take out a loan?"

Ray wondered why no one seemed to understand what he thought was a pretty simple request. He started talking slower.

"No. I don't need a loan. I have the money in my RRSP savings. I just want to take some of it out."

"But that's for your retirement," the advisor said.

"Precisely," Ray said. "And I'm retired. I simply want to take out some of my money."

The advisor searched through his desk for the correct form. "We'll have to withhold twenty percent for income taxes," he said.

Ray smiled. It looked like they were finally making some progress. "Yes, I know. The government always takes their cut."

"And there will be an admin charge of fifty dollars," Jim added.

"Excuse me?"

"There's an administration charge of fifty dollars every time money is transferred or withdrawn."

Ray's smile disappeared. "I'm not transferring my money to a different bank, and I'm not taking all of the money out and closing the account. I simply want some of the money – *my money* – to pay some extra bills. You mean you're going to charge me fifty bucks every time I want to take out some of *my* money?"

"I'm sorry, but it's our policy. We have to fill in some forms, so they charge an admin fee."

Ray could feel his anger rising. "You had to fill in forms when I put the money in too, but you didn't charge me any admin fee then. But you're telling me now you're going to charge me fifty bucks every time I want to take out some of my own damn money?"

The advisor's face went beet red. "Let me get my manager."

* * *

A few days later, Ray and his wife, Candice, were sitting in the office of Tim Forbes, a Certified Financial Planner. Rather than wearing a suit and tie like the guy at the bank, Tim was dressed in a casual shirt and looked more like a psychologist than an investment banker.

"I hear you're a little unhappy with your bank," Tim said.

"They want to charge me fifty bucks every time I want to take out some of my own damn money," Ray said. He recounted his experience with the bank.

"It's too bad you didn't get to talk to someone with a little more experience," Tim said. "The banks have qualified advisors, but they tend to hide them away except for their wealthiest customers."

"I'm not exactly poor," Ray said. "I haven't got a lot socked away into RRSP's, but I've got a good pension." He slid some papers across the desk to Tim so he could see his monthly pension income and how much he had in savings.

Tim took a quick look at the papers and jotted down some notes. Then he turned his focus to Candice.

"Mrs. Ferguson, how about yourself?"

"I worked full-time when I was younger, but then quit when our daughter, Amanda, was born. She's all grown up and married now with kids of her own. Over the last few years, I've worked a little bit at the library, but I didn't make much money."

"And how old are you now?"

"Sixty-four. I turn sixty-five month after next."

"So, you'll start drawing your CPP and OAS income pretty soon." Tim made a few more notes. "And Mr. Ferguson, how long have you been retired?"

"Almost two years now. It seemed time after I reached the thirty year mark with the police force."

"How do you like retirement so far?" Tim asked.

"It's been great," Ray said. "I get to play a lot more golf, which is my passion. We go to Florida for a couple of months in the winter. We went on a cruise together, two actually, which was great, but I'm not sure I want to do that again."

Tim noticed the last statement seemed to catch Candice by surprise.

"Mrs. Ferguson, how about you? Is retirement everything you hoped it would be?"

Candice gave a sideways glance toward Ray, looking a little unsure about how much info she should share. "I love to travel and I loved the two cruises we went on. It was so romantic exploring the Caribbean. I was hoping we'd be doing a lot more of them."

"We can't afford to keep going on cruises," Ray interjected.

Candice stiffened in her chair. "Isn't that what *he's* supposed to figure out?"

Tim moved the financial statements to the side of his desk. "Before we start looking at the money side of things, I think it's important that you both figure out what you *want* to do in your retirement years. It's only then that we start looking at the money side of things."

Tim grabbed a piece of paper from his desk, turned it sideways and drew a line across the bottom that extended across the entire page. "The first thing you have to realize is that your retirement is probably going to go on for another twenty-five years, possibly more if you're lucky enough to remain healthy." He wrote the current year on the left side of the line and the thirty year mark on the right side of the line, then drew intersecting lines about every five years.

"You're still in the first few years of your retirement – some people call this the honeymoon period – the time when you want to travel, take cruises, and golf until your arms fall off. But you can't be on a cruise ship twelve months of the year or golf every day. After a while, you'll get bored, even if you have enough money. I need you to start thinking about what you're going to do with yourself on a plain old Tuesday or Wednesday morning. Ray, you used to work forty hours a week."

"At least," Ray said.

"So you're going to have to find ways to use those newly found hours every week."

"What about me?" Candice asked. "I haven't worked full-time for years."

"I bet you still did something every day that made you feel valuable," Tim said.

Candice thought for a second. "I used to look after the kids for Amanda. She couldn't handle it on her own, especially with Tyler. But I'm not sure how much help I can be now. Now that Tyler's bigger, I don't think I can handle him anymore."

"Our grandson is autistic," Ray offered in explanation.

"I think both of you have experienced how important it is to *do* something every day," Tim said. "That doesn't change just because you're retired. That's why so many seniors volunteer at various social service agencies, or take up a new hobby like painting or music. I think you'll find that if you both just sit around the house, you'll start getting on each other's nerves."

Both Ray and Candice looked at each other, as if this guy had somehow been using video surveillance on them at their condo.

"I've always wanted to paint," Candice said in a half-whisper.

"I didn't know that," Ray said. "When have you ever painted?"

"I haven't," Candice said, "but I've always thought about it. I never seemed to have the time before."

Tim smiled. "Well guess what, *now* you've got the time."

* * *

It was about a week later when Ray and Candice met with the financial planner again. They had taken the timeline chart that Tim had sketched out for them at the last meeting and inserted planned activities into each five-year interval.

They had agreed to take one more cruise within the next five years, but had also inserted a trip to Europe.

"We both realized we wanted to see Paris at some point before we die," Candice said.

Tim noticed that Ray still had golf written down as his main activity in each five year interval, indicating he planned to golf five days a week now but gradually declining to once a week when he reached eighty-five years of age.

"To be honest, I have no idea what I'll feel like doing in twenty years," Ray said. "I'm just guessing."

"We all are," Tim said. "That's why I've broken it down into five-year intervals. Having a plan doesn't mean that you can't change it, but it sure beats the hell out of just winging it the whole way. We'll adjust the plan every year, looking at what you think you'll need now and what you think you'll need later."

"So, can we afford it?" Candice asked.

"I believe you can," Tim said, "but we'll have to keep a handle on some of the large expenditures, like the trip to Paris and purchasing a new car every four years. Ray's pension will cover all of your basic needs and a few of the extra fun things you want to do, but we'll also have to dip into your other holdings to pay for some of the extras."

A red flag seemed to go up for Ray. "I'm not sure I want you touching my pension," he said.

"I won't," Tim said, "although I think you can save some money in income tax by allocating some of your pension to Candice."

"What do you get out of all this?" Ray asked. "I doubt you're giving us all of this advice for free."

Tim smiled. "I'm not. I have to pay my bills too."

He explained that he would be transferring Ray's RRSP holdings from the bank to various investment funds. He'd be earning his fees by managing the investments.

"So you won't be charging me fifty bucks every time I want to take out some of my own money?" Ray asked.

"No," Tim said. "But I think we'll be trying to manage those withdrawals a little better."

* * *

When Max headed over to his father's place after his

day at the golf course, he was surprised to see his sister Karen waiting for him in the kitchen.

"What are we going to do about this?" she asked.

She pointed to a letter that had arrived that day in the mail. Max picked it up and saw it was an invoice from the hospital in Ohio that had treated his father on their way back from the Masters. The invoice was for just over eighteen thousand dollars, U.S. dollars.

"They said the insurance company denied the claim and now Dad has to pay it himself," Karen said.

"Denied the claim? Why?"

"They said Dad had an existing condition that wasn't disclosed on the application. Said he had a history of asthma."

"Dad's never had asthma," Max said. "What are they talking about?"

Karen shuffled through the papers on the table and pointed to an entry showing their father had been treated for asthma in a B.C. hospital.

"Dad's never even been to British Columbia," Max said as he picked up the paper. "There must be a mistake."

"Apparently he was," Karen said. "Back in 1982. I asked Dad about it and he said he and Mom had gone there on vacation. He said there were forest fires going on. There was smoke everywhere. He said he had trouble breathing so he went to the hospital. Lots of people in the area did. It wasn't asthma, but that's what shows up on the hospital report."

Max clenched his jaw. "For Christ's sake, that was over thirty years ago and it wasn't asthma. How can they call that a previous existing condition?"

Karen put her head in her hands. "Dad doesn't have any money and I certainly don't. What are we going to do?"

Max sighed and slumped down into a kitchen chair. "I have no idea."

* * *

The next day Max decided to call Stryker as he was the only lawyer he knew. He left a long-winded voice-mail describing the situation and hoped he would hear from him soon, as the letter from the hospital said they would begin legal action if payment wasn't received in thirty days. He was pleased when Stryker called him back later that morning.

"Don't worry about it," Stryker said. "Insurance companies do this all the time. They look for any reason they can find to deny a claim."

"So we shouldn't send the hospital any money?"

"No, you're going to have to give them something. What's the deductible on your father's policy?"

"I have no idea," Max said.

"It's probably five hundred or a thousand dollars. That's the norm for this type of policy. So, find out what that amount is and just send them that. No more, no less. You're going to have to pay that amount whatever the final outcome turns out to be."

"So who's going to pay the rest?"

"At this point, I don't know," Stryker said. "Once they realize you're not just going to roll over and pay the whole bill, the lawyers for the insurance company and the lawyers for the hospital usually negotiate the final payment amount. That'll take months."

"So we're off the hook?"

"Probably. I doubt the insurance company will come after you based on an argument of a pre-existing condition from over thirty years ago, but sometimes they do. If they try, give me another call."

"So how much do I owe you for the legal advice?"

"Nothing," Stryker said. "All I did was make a couple of phone calls. If they do decide to go to court over this, I'll have to refer you to another lawyer because I don't have the time to take this on. But I don't think you have anything to worry about."

CHAPTER 18: A MARATHON, NOT A SPRINT

As Cheech stood in line at Tim Horton's, he was feeling quite good about himself. Things had finally started to go in his favour again. Melanie had called earlier that morning to say they had signed the new advertising contract and the partners at NBT had come through with an offer of full-time employment. His new salary was almost forty thousand less than what he used to make, but that didn't matter. His lawyer had let him know a few days ago that his old company had agreed to give him their executive pension when he turned sixty-five. They had also offered up to four year's severance pay if he wasn't able to find another job. Part of the deal was that they'd top up his compensation if he had to accept a position at a lower salary. Cheech loved knowing that his old company would be paying forty grand a year to top up his salary from NBT.

When Cheech stepped out of Tim Horton's, he was approached by a pretty blonde woman wearing shorts and bright blue tee-shirt.

"I was wondering if I could talk you into sponsoring

me in this Sunday's run. It's to raise money for breast cancer research." She pointed to a pink ribbon on her shirt just beside a name tag that read "Susie", with a little heart dotting the "i" in her name.

This woman didn't need a pink ribbon to draw attention to her chest. Cheech's focus was already there. "I'm sure you could talk me into pretty much anything," he said.

Susie smiled, which highlighted the dimples in both of her cheeks. "It's a 10K run. You can sponsor me for each kilometer I run, or just specify a flat total amount."

Cheech looked at her sponsor sheet and saw a few people had sponsored her for twenty-five or fifty cents a kilometer, but most had simply specified a flat fee of five or ten dollars.

"I better specify a flat fee," Cheech said. He took a quick glance at her long, silky legs. "With legs like those, I have no doubt you'll run the full 10K." He wrote fifty dollars down on her sponsor sheet.

"Oh, thanks so much. You're so generous." She studied his physique. "Are you a runner?"

"Whenever I can," Cheech said.

That was an absolute lie. He hadn't run anywhere in over twenty years.

"You should come run with us on Sunday," Susie said. She touched Cheech's arm. "There's a bunch of us going to run together. You should join us. It'll be fun and they have a BBQ later for all of the runners and organizers."

Cheech's brain knew he should turn down the offer, but he wasn't thinking with his head at this point.

"I'll be there," he said.

* * *

Cheech was quite fortunate to find one of the last

parking spots in the lot beside the park where the 10K run was scheduled to start. It was a beautiful Sunday morning and the crowd was growing quickly. He wondered whether he'd even be able to find Susie in the hundreds of people milling around. She spotted him first.

"Cheech, Cheech, we're over here," she shouted.

Cheech turned toward the sound and saw her standing with several of her running mates. The two guys that were part of the group were young and muscular, obviously people who took their physical fitness seriously. The five women in the group were more varied. Two women looked to be in their late twenties, one of whom was pushing a toddler in a jogging stroller that had three large spoked wheels. One lady looked over forty and she was wearing a tee shirt that said she was a breast cancer survivor. Susie and the other woman were probably in their late thirties.

Cheech knew he would be the oldest one in Susie's group of friends and had been worried about it in the days leading up to the event. In fact, he'd started applying something to his hair over the last few days to see if it would reduce the amount of grey. The instructions on the box said there would be gradual change in his hair colour, but as far as he could tell, it hadn't done a damn thing.

Some participants in this event simply walked the course and didn't care how long it took them to complete it. Others were more competitive and were always trying to better their times. Cheech could tell that Susie's group were the competitive type.

Susie pulled him aside and whispered in his ear. "We'll probably run a little slower than you're used to." She pointed to the older lady in the breast cancer survivor tee-shirt. "Barb isn't normally part of our group, but she asked if she could run with us today. We're going to let her set the pace. This run is really important to her."

"No problem," Cheech said. "We're just out here to have fun and raise money."

For the first kilometer, Cheech found the pace quite comfortable and used the opportunity to chat up Susie while they were running. The organizers had water stations positioned every kilometer along the route, but the group didn't give the first rest stop any consideration and kept on running.

When they reached the second water station, Barb signaled she needed a break and the group stopped to grab some water. The two young guys continued to jog on the spot, but Cheech took the opportunity to catch his breath. His lungs were starting to burn and his left quad muscle was starting to object to this new activity. He now wished he exercised on a more regular basis. Barb took two quick gulps of water and signaled to the group she was ready to go again.

For the next two kilometers, Cheech found it difficult to keep up with the group, but he continued to push himself. He was so out of breath, he could no longer continue to chat with Susie while they ran.

The kid in the stroller started to kick up a fuss when they reached the half-way point. His mother stopped to see what the problem was. The two young guys in the group decided to keep going, but Cheech decided to stay with the ladies.

"Are you okay?" Susie asked Cheech when she saw his face. "You don't look so good."

"I might have tweaked my left quad," Cheech said, "but it's nothing to worry about. I'll be fine."

He was lying. Everything was hurting now and he was glad the toddler had forced them to stop.

"Problem solved," the toddler's mother said a few seconds later. "Let's go."

The group started up again. Shortly after, Cheech knew he was in trouble. He desperately wanted to stop, but didn't know how to do so without losing face. *Hell, I can't even keep up with a bunch of women anymore, including one who's pushing a goddamn stroller.* He considered grabbing his quad muscle and faking an injury, but that just seemed pathetic.

Suddenly he felt something hit his right leg. He looked down to see that the lace on his right shoe had come undone and the long lace was hitting his leg on every stride. That seemed like a legitimate excuse to stop for a breather.

"My shoe," he said to Susie, pointing to his foot.

He stepped off the right side of the path onto the grass. He wasn't sure how much time he could milk out of this minor setback. He took the shoe off completely and pretended to dump a stone out of it, even though there was nothing inside. Then he slowly put the shoe back on and bent over to do up the laces again, this time in a double knot.

When he stood up again, he suddenly felt dizzy and nauseous. He couldn't regain his focus and felt like he was staring directly into the sun.

"Are you okay?" Susie asked.

That's the last thing he heard before he hit the ground.

* * *

When Cheech woke up, he found himself in the emergency room at the hospital with EKG pads on his chest and legs and an IV stuck into his arm. He vaguely remembered Susie hovering over him on the grass and the ambulance ride to the hospital, but he had kept drifting in and out.

"Welcome back," someone said. He turned to see a woman sitting in the chair beside his bed. It was his wife, Maggie.

"What are you doing here?" Cheech asked.

"The hospital called me. You still have me down as your emergency contact."

Cheech scanned the room to see if there was anyone else around.

"If you're looking for your little playmate, she's down the hall," Maggie said. "I think she's talking to the cute paramedic that brought you in. Her name's Susie, right?"

"We're just running mates," Cheech said.

"So is that what the kids are calling it today? Anyway, we had a nice little chat. Apparently, you neglected to tell her you had a wife."

"Remember, we're separated. The topic of my marital status never came up."

"I'm sure it didn't."

Just then, the curtain around his bed opened and a nurse came in. She was an older, hefty-looking woman. Her name tag indicated her name was Clara.

"So I see our runner is back with us," Clara said.

"Yeah, he woke up a few minutes ago, but I don't think he's going to be running again anytime soon," Maggie said.

"Probably a good thing," Clara said. "We got your test results back and the doc says your heart is fine. However, your blood sugar level isn't. When's the last time you ate something?"

"I don't remember," Cheech said.

"Don't you lie to me," the nurse said. "You didn't eat any breakfast before you started your little marathon, did you?"

"No," Cheech admitted.

Clara turned to Maggie. "Why did you let him out of the house this morning without anything to eat?"

"He's not my responsibility anymore," Maggie said. "We're separated."

"Oh," Clara said, looking confused for a few seconds. She pointed her finger at Maggie and then out toward the hallway. "So the little cutie down the hall is his..."

"Running mate," Maggie said.

"Ahhh," Clara said, exchanging a nod with Maggie.

She turned toward Cheech and started disconnecting the cables from the EKG pads. "This might hurt a little bit." She proceeded to remove one of the pads from Cheech's chest, ripping a large patch of hair off his chest in the process.

"Ow!" Cheech screamed.

"Don't be such a baby," Clara said. She seemed to be enjoying this. She ripped the other pads off his chest with equal vigor. "I think it's about time you grew up and started acting your age. Maybe cut down on your running around."

Just then, the curtain opened and Susie poked her head in. "Cheech, if you're going to be okay, I think I'm going to be heading off now."

Several awkward looks were exchanged between everyone in the room. Eventually, all eyes turned their focus to Cheech. "Yeah, that's probably best," he said. "I'm sorry. This was all my fault."

Susie didn't say a word, but just closed the curtain and hurried off down the hall.

The nurse turned to Maggie. "We're probably going to release him within the next few hours. Are you going to drive him home or should we just send him home in a taxi?"

"Legally, I guess he's still my responsibility," Maggie said. She sighed. "Someone's got to take care of him."

CHAPTER 19: LEAGUE PLAY

Ladies Day was held every Tuesday during the summer at Riverview.   Men were also allowed to play golf on Tuesdays, but the prime morning tee times were reserved for the women, something which annoyed the men immensely.

The women who signed up for ladies league would compete for a weekly prize, but they also accumulated points throughout the year for an overall winner. Some women were quite competitive, while others just enjoyed the social aspects of the game.

Since this particular Tuesday was a bright summer day, the pro shop was surrounded by forty or fifty women, all bubbling with enthusiasm and sharing the latest gossip or discussing last night's episode of *"Dancing With The Stars"*.

In the middle of them all was Norm. Norm was a silver-haired man who only worked a few days a week in the pro shop, but he normally drew the Tuesday shifts for a few reasons. One was that most of the other staff avoided Tuesdays like the plague, as they couldn't stand the chaos of Ladies Day. But the main reason was that he was a real charmer and all of the ladies loved him.

"Good morning, Norm," Ally said as she pulled up in her golf cart.

"Hooray, Ally's here!" Norm shouted when he saw her. "How's my favourite girl doing this morning?"

"Bright eyed and bushy-tailed." She got out of her cart to give Norm a hug.

"Don't get me going by getting me thinking about your back end," Norm said as he gave her butt a little pat.

"Oh, stop it!" Ally said, but it was apparent she didn't really mind.

All of the staff at Riverview had been instructed to treat the members with the upmost respect and courtesy. They were to be addressed as Mister or Missus this, or Doctor that. But those rules didn't seem to apply to Norm.

Ally pointed to the younger woman sitting in her golf cart. "Norm, this is my daughter Angie. She's visiting with me for the next few days, so I thought I'd bring her out golfing."

Angie reached out to shake Norm's hand, but he lifted her hand up to his lips and kissed it. "I see good looks run in the family."

"Down boy," Ally said. "She's already married and much, much too young for you. If you're looking for someone to fool around with, you should try someone your own age."

Norm noticed that Jerry was heading over toward them. "Uh-oh, here comes Jerry. That probably means you're next on the tee."

Ally waved to Jerry. "It's okay. I know we're next. Just let me grab some water and we'll be right there." She did so, then jumped back in her cart and raced down the path to the first tee."

When they got there, Ally noticed that her daughter was looking at her with a big smile on her face. "What are you grinning about?"

"Nothing," Angie said. "I've just never seen you act that way before. What's the story with you and Norm?"

"Oh, we just tease each other. There's nothing going on."

"It's okay, Mom. Dad passed away over four years ago now. Your only sixty-three. I think it would be great if you had a new man in your life. Is he married?"

"I have no idea. Besides, we're just flirting. He does it with all of the girls."

Angie raised an eyebrow. "I don't know. I think I detected a little chemistry there."

Ally could feel her face start to flush. "You really think so?" She thought for a second. "He does make me feel something I haven't felt for a few years."

Angie reached down and took a drink of her water. "Special?"

"Horny."

Water came flying out of Angie's mouth and nose. "Mother, I can't believe you just said that."

"Hey, I'm just old. I'm not dead yet."

* * *

Men's League was held every Wednesday, following a similar points-based system used by the ladies. Sure, there were some who participated for the social aspect, but most of the guys took the competition much more seriously than the ladies did.

The real competition happened in all of the side bets. In the skins game, if you happened to be the only one out of all of the golfers to birdie a particular hole that day, you could take home a good chunk of change.

There were also multiple sub-groups, each with their own little mini-competitions. The "Top 20" consisted of some, but not all, of the best golfers at the club. The "Bionic Men" were guys who had hips or knees replaced. And the "Beach Boys" were guys who were known more for their parties than their golfing ability. To be fair, most of the guys went for a drink after their round, but members of the "Beach Boys" would still be in the clubhouse several hours after their rounds were completed.

The pros at the club would sometimes play with the guys on Wednesdays. It was a good way to stay connected with the members. Max had put his name in to play that day with Ray Ferguson and Bruce Thompson, but it wasn't just a social game. He had an agenda, but he had to wait for the right moment.

"How's your grandson doing?" Max asked Ray.

"Much better," Ray said. "Amanda and her husband managed to get him into a program for autistic kids. It's only two days a week, but it seems to be helping. They're going to be coming to visit us in a few weeks."

"We're running a kids golf camp around then," Max said. "You should bring them out for it."

"Oh, I don't know. We'll probably bring Elizabeth over, but I'm not sure Tyler's ready for something like that."

"You never know until you try," Max said.

Max turned his attention to Bruce. "How are the twins doing?"

"Great," Bruce said. "I think the kids are finally launched out into the world. Emma got a full-time job, but it took her over six months to find it. A degree is no longer a guarantee of getting a good job."

"What about Josh?"

"He's doing well. Got himself a new girlfriend. She's a golfer. They're both members over at Blackhawk Ridge."

This provided Max with an easy segue into what he really wanted to talk about. "I see that both of you have already qualified for the Challenge Cup team. I've decided I'm going to captain the team myself this year. It's going to be quite a challenge with Stryker now playing for the other side."

"Yeah, Stryker always seems to do well in match play," Bruce said.

"Our ladies seem pretty strong," Max said. "Thanks for talking Marilyn into playing."

Bruce's wife was a pretty good golfer, but she normally didn't like playing in competitions. She was just in it for the fun.

"I'm more worried about the strength of our men's team," Max continued. "I noticed Cheech hasn't even tried to qualify. I was hoping he would."

"He's got himself a new job," Bruce explained, "so I'm not sure how much time he's got for golf right now."

"You guys still play with him, don't you?" Max asked.

"Not too much," Ray said, "but we're playing with him on Friday. He said he can sometimes sneak off early at the end of the week to get a round in."

"Would you mind encouraging him to try to qualify for this year's team? I'm trying to recruit our best players and I think he'd be a real asset."

* * *

Riverview held a Junior Golf Camp in the middle of the summer since a lot of the members had grandkids visiting them at that time. It had grown to be quite a popular event over the years, which meant it was all-hands-on-deck for the staff. Max had just finished the early morning staff meeting and was coming out of his office when he saw his sister Karen come into the pro shop.

"Karen, what are you doing here? Is Dad okay?"

"He's fine, but his caregiver called to cancel this morning and I didn't want to leave him on his own." She pointed to their father who was standing outside the pro shop. "I was hoping he could just hang around the golf course with you for the day."

Max shook his head. "This wasn't part of our deal. I keep an eye on him at nights and you and the nurse look after him during the day."

"I know," Karen said, "but I'm driving a bunch of other teachers to Toronto this morning for a seminar. I'm already late. The caregiver only called about twenty minutes ago to cancel, so I'm stuck."

"So am I," Max said. "We've got the Junior Golf Camp this morning. The kids are already starting to arrive." He pointed to a few of the early arrivals.

"Dad's good with kids," Karen said. "Maybe he can help. I'm sorry, but I've got to go."

She bolted from the pro shop and was gone before Max could offer any more objections. Max headed outside to find his father.

"What's with all the kids?" his father said when he saw him.

"It's the first day of our Junior Golf Camp," Max said. He pointed to a golf cart that was parked close to the pro shop. "Dad, why don't you just sit in the cart here while we get everything organized?" Max helped his father over to the golf cart.

Just then, Scott started calling out the names of the kids registered for the camp. He ticked each of their names off on a clipboard he was holding when they responded.

"Tyler Armstrong," Scott shouted. There was no response. He called his name again.

"That's my grandson," Ray Ferguson said. "He's over on the putting green with my granddaughter, Elizabeth. She should be on your list as well."

Scott ticked both their names off on his list.

Max knew that Tyler was Ray's autistic grandson and was glad that Ray had decided to bring him. Both Tyler and Elizabeth were on the far side of the putting green, away from all of the other kids. He watched as Tyler putted the ball into the hole from a few feet away, picked it out of the hole and then repeated it again and again.

Ray came over to talk to Max. "If it's alright with you, I'm going to hang around and watch to make sure Tyler is okay."

They normally wanted the parents and grandparents to leave as soon as they dropped off their kids, but Max knew that Ray was worried about him. "I'm sure he'll be fine," Max said, but Ray still hovered close by.

After all of the kids were checked in, the staff marched them all in single file toward the practice range. Tyler and Elizabeth followed along about ten paces behind the other kids.

When they got to the range, the staff had each of the kids spread out across the tee, each with a small bucket of golf balls beside them. Scott told each of them to pull out a 7-iron or whatever short iron they had brought with them. Some of the kids had a full set of clubs; others only had two or three clubs with them.

Scott stood in front of the group and instructed them on the proper way to grip the club. There were about twenty kids in the golf camp and four instructors, so each instructor would watch over the handful of kids closest to them to make sure they were doing it correctly. Then Scott showed them the basics of how to make a golf swing, first just trying to hit the ground without a ball being there.

Tyler and Elizabeth were the last two kids in the line of golfers. Although Max normally just supervised the entire group, he decided to move his golf cart down toward them so he could keep a closer eye on Tyler.

Elizabeth was following instructions perfectly and had a pretty good golf swing. Tyler was just swinging his club in the air around in circles. Max got out of the golf cart and slowly approached Tyler. He tried to get Tyler to swing the club so it hit the ground, but Tyler continued to just swing it in the air. He seemed to be having fun and he was far enough away from everyone that he wasn't going to hit anyone with his club, so Max just let him continue.

Next, Scott told the kids to put a ball in front of them and see if they could hit the ball. Most of them missed completely on their first few attempts, then would top the ball so it only went a few yards, but a few eventually managed to make contact with the ball.

Max pulled a ball from the bucket, placed it on the ground in front of Tyler and told him to try to hit it. He was surprised when Tyler made contact on his first attempt. *Probably beginners luck.*

Tyler grabbed another ball from the bucket, placed it on the ground in front of him and took another swing. This time the ball rocketed off the club face and flew about twenty yards.

Max noticed that Tyler was standing with his feet together. He put another ball in front of him and then moved his feet so he had a wider stance. Tyler swung again and the ball flew about fifty yards and landed beside one of the target flags on the range. Tyler grabbed another ball from the bucket and did it again. And again.

One of the other instructors looked over to see who was hitting all of these shots and was surprised to see it was Tyler. He stopped to watch, and then a few of the other kids stopped to watch as well. Eventually, everyone was focused on this little kid who seemed to hit the ball solidly every time.

"I haven't seen anyone hit a ball like that since Moe Norman," Max said to his father.

"Moe who?"

"Moe Norman. He was a pro from Kitchener. Some of the top golfers say he was the best ball striker in the world, ever. He might have been autistic too."

They watched as Tyler hit the entire bucket of balls. They all landed within a few feet of the target flag. When the bucket was empty, Tyler smiled. Then he started swinging the club around in the air again.

One of the staff started putting more balls into the bucket in front of Tyler.

"Don't put too many in there," Max warned. "I don't think he'll stop until they're all gone."

Sure enough, when Tyler saw there were more golf balls in his bucket, he started hitting them again with the same precision that he had before.

* * *

It was about an hour later when Amanda and Doug arrived to pick up Tyler and Elizabeth. Ray had gone home to get them because he wanted them to see what Tyler could do.

All of the other kids had already gone home, but Tyler was still out on the range. Max had spent the rest of the

147

morning working with Tyler. With his parents watching, Max showed how Tyler could hit short irons or long irons. He had even shown Tyler how to put a ball on a tee so he could hit a driver.

His mother, Amanda, had tears in her eyes.

His father was bursting with pride. "I didn't know he could do anything like that," he said.

Max turned and whispered to them. "Sometimes, I think it's good to see the spectrum differently. I think we all get too focused on what he can't do, rather than trying to discover what he can."

* * *

As Max drove his father back home after their long day at the golf course, he noticed his father was being awfully quiet.

"What are you thinking about?" Max asked.

"I was wrong," his father said.

"About what?"

"All these years, I thought that those who can, do. Those who can't, teach. I thought you'd never reached your full potential, that you should have been a touring pro. But when I saw you with those kids today, I saw what a good teacher you are."

"Well, Tyler's a special case. I can't take credit for him."

"Not just with him. I saw how you worked with all of the kids and their parents. I think maybe you're exactly where you should be." He turned to look at Max. "I'm proud of you."

Max had been waiting his whole life to hear that.

CHAPTER 20: BLACK FRIDAY

The following Friday, Cheech showed up for his golf game with Ray Ferguson and Bruce Thompson. He headed toward the blue tees, the ones they normally used.

"Hold up there," Bruce shouted to him. "We're back here today. It's Black Friday."

Riverview had five sets of tees on each hole, with each set in a different colour. Golfers were advised to play from whichever tee suited their ability. The red tees were the farthest forward and used to be referred to as the ladies tees, but male members who were over eighty years old also used them. The white tees were a little farther back and were used by the players who couldn't hit the ball very far. About a third of the guys normally played from those tees, but a few of the ladies who were good golfers also preferred to play from the whites. The blue tees were a little further back and were used by most of the men. Even further back were the gold tees.

The black tees were where professionals or top amateurs would play from and this was sometimes referred to as "playing from the tips". These tees were rarely used, but a few of the guys had started playing from them on Fridays. It became known as "Black Friday".

As Cheech stood on the first tee, he quickly realized the course looked entirely different from the black tees. The sand trap on the left side of the fairway that he would normally clear with ease suddenly became a problem. He aimed his tee shot to the right to avoid the trap. His second shot came up short of the green and he ended up making a bogey. In fact, he made bogies on four of the first five holes.

"I'm not sure I'll break a hundred from back here," Cheech said when they reached the sixth tee.

"It certainly takes some getting used to," Bruce said, "but it's fun to challenge yourself sometimes."

Ray took that as his cue. "Speaking of challenging yourself, we were wondering why you haven't tried qualifying for the Challenge Cup team yet. We could sure use you on the team this year."

"You think I'm good enough to make the team?"

"You should make it easily," Bruce said. "You're given three chances to qualify and they take your best two rounds out of three."

"We don't have to play from the tips when we qualify, do we?"

"No. You can use whatever tees you want. Most of the guys play from the blues."

For the next few holes, both Bruce and Ray continued to encourage him to try out for the team.

"It's really important to Max," Bruce said. "Blackhawk Ridge has kicked our ass for the last few years and Max wants to turn it around. It'll be even harder this year with Stryker playing for them."

As they continued playing, Cheech started getting used to playing the course from the tips. He had made a string of pars and even managed to make a birdie on the par five thirteenth hole.

"Now this is a scary shot," Cheech said when he reached the fifteenth tee. When he played this hole from the blue tees, he would normally hit an iron off the tee to make sure he found the fairway. There was a huge water hazard in front of the tee that extended down the left side. Out of bounds was down the right side. From the black tees, Cheech knew he'd have to hit a long straight drive just to hit dry land. "I don't normally do well on these pressure shots."

"I find the key is to visualize a positive outcome," Bruce said to encourage him. "Then just grip it and rip it."

"These are the shots that really test what you're made of," Ray said. "So let's see what you've got."

Cheech closed his eyes and imagined his tee shot clearing the water and landing in the fairway. Then he confidently stepped up to the ball and hit a perfect tee shot. It easily cleared the water and bounded down the fairway.

"Geez that felt good," Cheech said. "I wish I could hit them all like that."

"I knew you could come through under pressure," Bruce said.

Cheech was absolutely pumped. "You can tell Max I'm going to try out for the team."

* * *

Jessica had arrived at around seven that morning for her shift at Shady Oaks. One of her duties was to help the residents get out of bed, get dressed and ready for breakfast. She enjoyed this part of the day as most of the elderly residents were at their best in the mornings. Some woke up as early as four-thirty, so were already dressed by the time she arrived.

"It's time to rise and shine," she said when she entered Shirley's room. She was surprised to see that Shirley was still in bed. She was normally one of the early risers.

Jessica pulled the curtains open and sunshine spilled into the room. When Shirley didn't move or make a sound, Jessica immediately knew something was wrong. She pulled the cord beside the bed to call for assistance.

Elena arrived a few seconds later and immediately assessed the situation. "Call the doctor."

Jessica froze. She heard Elena's instructions, but for some reason, couldn't move.

Elena reached over and pushed the button for the intercom. "We need a doctor in room 18, stat."

Jessica still couldn't move. She watched Elena check Shirley for vital signs. There didn't appear to be any.

A few minutes later, the doctor arrived and took over trying to revive Shirley, to no avail. Several other staff also appeared.

"Get her out of here," Elena said, pointing at Jessica.

Emily, one of the other volunteers, took Jessica's elbow and led her out of the room. She walked her to a small loveseat that was just down the hallway and helped her sit down.

Since Jessica had been working for several months at Shady Oaks, this was not the first medical emergency she had seen. A few residents had even died. But this was the first time Jessica had been the first to discover the body. Sure, she never seemed to remember Jessica's name, or anyone else's for that matter, but Shirley had always taken a shine to her. And because no family ever came to visit Shirley, Jessica spent extra time with her and she had become her favourite resident.

Jessica watched as several people came and went from Shirley's room: Elena, the doctor, and then a priest. A few of the other residents stopped by and tried to peer into Shirley's room, but they were quickly led away. Jerry seemed particularly upset when he arrived and went into her room. A little later on, someone from the funeral home arrived to remove the body. Jessica continued to sit in the hallway watching, seemingly unable to move.

Elena came over and sat down beside her. "How are you doing?"

"I'm okay, a little numb."

"That's to be expected. I know you'd grown quite close to Shirley."

"Yeah, I suppose I shouldn't do that, cause it hurts too much when they go."

"It just means you care and that's the most important thing. I think that's why you're going to be a great nurse. These are people, not just patients."

Jessica wiped away the tears on her cheeks. "Does it ever get any easier?"

"I wish it did. If it does, then it probably means it's time to move on and do something else."

Jessica sighed. "Shirley was such a sweetheart. I think I was drawn to her even more because she didn't have any family around her."

"That's where you're wrong." Elena took Jessica's hand. "Here, come with me."

She led her down the hall to Shirley's room. Inside, Jerry was starting to gather up all of Shirley's belongings. He reached inside one of the cupboards and pulled out a small bag that had some small framed pictures inside it. He pulled one out that looked to be about twenty years old and stared at it.

"Is that you in the picture with Shirley?" Jessica asked.

Jerry turned, his eyes red from tears. "Yes, yes it is."

Elena touched Jessica's shoulder. "You see, Shirley wasn't alone. She did have her family around her. Jerry's her husband."

"But, but..." Jessica stammered in confusion. "I thought you were just one of the volunteers."

"That's the cruel thing about dementia," Elena said. "When Shirley first came to us, Jerry used to visit her every day. So did a lot of her friends. But after a while, she stopped remembering who they were. The friends stopped coming, but Jerry always came. It used to upset Shirley when we told her she was married to Jerry because she didn't remember him. Eventually, we decided to just tell her he was one of our volunteers."

"I could tell the two of you had some kind of chemistry together," Jessica said. "But how could that be if she didn't even know who you are?"

"I can't explain it," Elena said. "Maybe it's because the heart always remembers, even if the brain doesn't."

Jessica turned toward Jerry. "It must have been so hard for you. Did she not remember you at all?"

"Most of the time, no, but every now and then something would trigger her memory."

Jessica thought for a second. "Like with the snow globe."

"Yes, the Bessborough Hotel in Saskatoon. That's where we had our wedding reception."

"Why didn't you just tell me?"

"When people knew, they were always trying to get her to remember things from her past," Elena said. "That just got her more and more upset. Eventually, we decided to tell people that Jerry was just a volunteer here. There were only a few of us who knew the whole story."

Jessica turned to Jerry and gave him a hug. "I'm so

sorry for you. What are you going to do now?"

"The funeral will be next week. Then I'm going to take Shirley home to Saskatchewan. After that, I don't know."

"Well you're always welcome here," Elena said.

* * *

Jerry ran the chamois over the camper-van one last time before backing it out of the garage. Shirley's funeral had been held just over a week ago and it was time to take her ashes back home to Saskatchewan. Jerry had decided to drive rather than fly. This was the trip they had always talked about taking when Jerry retired, something that he'd continually delayed, trying to work a few extra years to top up his pension. He now realized that the time they'd lost was worth much more than the extra money. By the time he finally retired, her health had already started to go downhill.

He glanced over to the passenger seat to see the urn with her ashes securely fastened in by the seat belt. He had placed a pillow on the seat to make her ride more comfortable and also so she'd sit a little higher. He now regretted the times he had teased her about being "vertically challenged".

He headed north up through the Muskokas, describing the pink and grey outcroppings of granite, the towering trees and the sparkling lakes to Shirley along the way. When he reached Sudbury, he made sure to show Shirley the "Big Nickel", the 30-foot replica of a 1951 Canadian nickel before finding a motel for the night.

He woke up early the next morning and continued on to Wawa, where he showed her the huge statue of a majestic Canada Goose. Their next stop was in White River, the birthplace of the famous bear, *Winnie the Pooh*.

Jerry continued the drive each day through the rest of Ontario and Manitoba, describing what he saw to his wife along the way.

When he reached Saskatchewan, he headed up through Saskatoon. He decided to spend the night in the Bessborough Hotel for old times' sake.

The next day, he headed north through Prince Albert toward Emma Lake. It was a hot summer day and the beach was filled with kids and their families swimming and playing games in the clear water. Jerry parked the camper-van under a tree and listened to the sounds of people having fun.

In the late afternoon, the heat and humidity built up into a series of thunderstorms. The beach was quickly evacuated, with the patrons racing home to their cabins or campers. Jerry stayed right where he was. The sound of the rain on the roof of the camper-van seemed soothing.

After the storm was over, Jerry carefully undid the seat belt, picked up the urn and walked down toward the dock. The storm had chased most people away, so there was hardly anyone around.

He headed into the little store on the dock that sold ice cream, drinks and candy. They also rented out canoes and small boats.

"How much to rent a small boat?" Jerry asked the kid behind the counter. The kid looked to be about sixteen years old with spiked hair and far too many tattoos on his arms.

"No more rentals today," the kid said without even looking up. "Cuz of the storm."

An older man who was busy restocking the fridges with pop looked up to see Jerry. He noticed the urn under Jerry's arm. "Is that what I think it is?"

Jerry didn't answer the question. "I just need a boat, any kind of a boat, just for a little while. I won't be long."

The kid behind the counter still didn't look up. "No more rentals today," he repeated.

Jerry looked at the older man. "Please."

The man placed the last of the cans of pop in the fridge. "You can take the row boat at the end of the dock."

"Thank you," Jerry said. "How much?"

The man just waved his hand. "Just take it."

Jerry nodded his thanks and headed out of the store. He placed the urn on the edge of the dock while he climbed down into the boat. He untied the rope from the mooring and then carefully retrieved the urn and placed it in between his feet on the bottom of the boat.

It had been years since he'd rowed a boat, but he quickly got the hang of it again. He rowed out into the lake and then headed towards a little alcove that seemed like the perfect place. He remembered how Shirley had said that the lake was the perfect place to get away from it all, the perfect place to think, the perfect place to rest.

They had agreed years ago that they both wanted to be cremated and their ashes scattered, not stuck in a jar or buried in the ground. He opened the top of the urn and paused. He felt like he should say a prayer or something, but he wasn't a religious man, so he had no idea what to say.

He slowly poured the ashes into the water and watched as they floated away. Then he dropped the urn over the side and into the water. He never felt so alone in his life. She had been the love of his life and now she was gone. How would he ever go on without her?

He sat in the boat for quite a while, not making a sound. Finally he found the strength to pick up the oars and started rowing back towards the dock. As he got out of the boat, he looked back out into the lake. The storm had now passed and the setting sun glistened over the lake. That's why they called it Sunset Bay. As the mist rose, a rainbow appeared over the little alcove. It was only there for a few seconds before it was gone again. It was almost as if the heavens had reached down and pulled her up.

Shirley had come home.

CHAPTER 21: THE RESCUE CLUB

When Jerry arrived back in Ontario, he spent several days just sitting around the house. Although he had lived in the house alone for several years, ever since Shirley had moved to Shady Oaks, it seemed even quieter than ever now. It took him a few days to realize that the clock in the kitchen above the sink had stopped. The steady tick-tock indicator of time marching on had been silenced. *Batteries must have died.* He didn't feel stable enough to stand on a chair to reach up and put new ones in. He felt like the earth was shifting underneath his feet.

A few days later, he headed into Shady Oaks. Elena had called inviting him back, saying all of the residents and staff had been asking about him. But when he got there, he simply made the rounds to say goodbye to everyone. There were too many painful memories to return to work there. He knew his days volunteering at Shady Oaks were over. He returned home, alone, again.

He wished they'd had kids. At first, Jerry had put it off saying he wanted to get his life in order first. Get a good job, buy a house, save some money. You know, build a stable environment before bringing a kid into the world. Shirley had been so patient with him, willing to wait until everything was perfect. When they finally decided it was time to *"pull the goalie"* and try to have a baby, it just never happened. They figured it was never meant to be. It didn't matter; they'd have each other for the rest of their lives, right?

Wrong.

It was a few days later when Jerry heard a knock on his door. He was surprised to see who it was.

"Hi Max. What brings you by?"

"Just wanted to stop in and see how you're doing." Max was carrying two coffees from Tim Horton's.

Jerry invited him in. "Okay, I guess. It's taking me a little longer than I expected to get my feet back under me."

Max placed the coffee on the kitchen table. "I wasn't sure how you take your coffee, so I just asked them for black and you can dress it up however you like." Max reached into his pocket, pulled out several creamers and packets of sugar and scattered them on the table.

Jerry loved the smell of coffee. It had been several days since he'd bothered to get one. "Thanks. I'm a double-double man." He proceeded to add the cream and sugar.

Max sat down at the table. "I know I told you to take as much time as you need, but I was wondering when you think you'll be back at work. The place is starting to fall apart without you. Everyone's been asking about you."

Max reached into his back pocket, pulled out two envelopes and slid them across the table toward Jerry.

Jerry opened the first envelope and saw it was a card signed by the staff offering their condolences. The second card was from the members. He was surprised by how many people had signed it and how many had written personalized messages.

"Thanks," Jerry said. "This means a lot."

"The club members consider you part of their family. We all do."

Jerry continued to read the messages on the cards. He was starting to feel a little overwhelmed and afraid he was going to start to cry.

Max rescued him. "Look, next Tuesday is Ladies Day again and I don't think we can get through another one without you. Scott filled in as starter last week but he lost all control. I'm pretty sure he just gave up and hid in the back shop until they all left. We need you back."

Jerry smiled. He could picture Scott trying to get all of the women organized and off the first tee.

"Sure, I'll be there next Tuesday."

* * *

Jerry had set an alarm for the crack of dawn the following Tuesday morning, but he didn't really need it. He was out of bed before it went off. It felt good to have something to do, to have a purpose, to be needed.

As he sat at the kitchen table eating his breakfast, he looked up at the clock to check the time. He still hadn't put in new batteries. He searched the drawer by the fridge until he found a package of new ones. Then he slid his chair over, climbed up and put the new batteries in.

Tick-tock, tick-tock.

Time was moving forward again.

* * *

When Jerry arrived at the golf course, there seemed to be even more chaos than normal. All of the ladies, every last one of them, gave him a hug and offered their condolences, but then they quickly moved on to their demands.

"I'm scheduled to play with Bev, but Bev is only going to play nine today – her daughter's getting married this weekend and Bev is organizing a bridal shower later tonight – so I was thinking that we'd move Bev up into Judy's group and then move Irene back into Bev's group, but since Irene shares a cart with Gladys, we'll have to bump Sandra into Heather's group – but I think that'll work cause they're both walkers. Is that okay?"

Jerry was madly marking the changes on his tee sheet. "Yes, I think that'll work."

He scanned the faces of the women surrounding him until he found the person he was looking for. "Judy, your group is next on the tee. Ladies, let's keep things moving."

The chaos continued for the rest of the morning and didn't slow down until after two in the afternoon. Jerry felt good about the day, but was exhausted by then. His back was feeling the strain of standing all day and he was resting in a golf cart by the starter's podium.

He saw Anne-Marie drive up in her cart and he checked her time on the tee sheet. She was scheduled to play at 2:52 with Janet. Jerry should have gotten up to greet her, but he lacked the energy. Anne-Marie came over and sat down in the seat beside him.

"I'm early," Anne-Marie said. "Any sign of Janet yet?"

"No, but your tee time is not for another thirty minutes. She usually doesn't show up until about ten minutes before."

Anne-Marie reached over and touched his hand. "Sorry to hear about your wife. How are you holding up?"

"Okay, I guess. It's tough dealing with the loneliness."

"I know all about that. I lost Bill a few years ago. One thing that really helped me was something the minister said. He said *Don't think of him as gone, think of him as gone ahead.*"

"I'm not sure I understand," Jerry said.

"Well, we moved here from out west. Bill moved here first when he got a new job, then I came a couple of months later after he got settled. I was lonely being left behind at the start, but I knew I'd eventually be joining him again. It made it bearable."

She reached over to pat his hand. "So, think of it as your wife has simply gone ahead to get things settled. When the time is right, you'll be joining her again."

Jerry thought for a second. She was right. That did make it feel a little better.

* * *

Cheech was on the driving range trying out a new 3-hybrid which he'd borrowed from the pro shop. Max had recommended it after Cheech had complained about having trouble hitting shots out of the rough. Max accompanied him over to the range to offer his assistance.

"Do I hit this thing like a 3-wood?" Cheech asked.

"No," Max said. "You hit your 3-wood with a sweeping motion. The shaft of a 3-wood is longer than a hybrid and is great from the fairway because you'll get greater distance. You actually hit a hybrid like an iron, hitting down on the ball."

"Okay, so then what's the difference between a 3-iron and a 3-hybrid?" Cheech asked.

Max grabbed a 3-iron from Cheech's bag and placed it beside the 3-hybrid. "The length of the shafts of both clubs is pretty much the same, but the club heads are quite a bit different. The 3-iron is more like a blade whereas the hybrid has a bigger head on it, but not as big as a 3-wood."

"Will that make it go farther?" Cheech asked.

"Maybe a little," Max said, "but usually not too much. Why don't you hit a few to compare?"

Cheech hit a few shots with his 3-iron. The balls came flying off the club face with a fairly low trajectory.

"Now try the hybrid," Max said.

The shots went about the same distance, but they flew higher in the air.

"That's because hybrids have a lower and deeper centre of gravity." Max said. "You may find them a little more forgiving if you hit it a little off the toe or the heel of the club."

"I'm usually okay from the fairway," Cheech said. "It's when I'm hitting out of the rough that I'm having problems."

Max grabbed a few balls from the bucket and headed over to the side of the range, where the grass was a little longer. He threw three balls down in the longer grass. "Let's see you hit these with your 3-iron."

The first one that Cheech hit was almost perfect, going just as long and straight as the ones from the short grass. But the second one only got about ten feet in the air and hooked to the left.

"The long grass grabbed the club and closed the club face on that one," Cheech said.

"Now try it with the hybrid," Max said.

Cheech hit three shots in a row that all went higher and straighter.

"That's why they're called rescue clubs," Max said. "They're great out of the short rough. Straighter, higher, almost like you're hitting from the fairway. If you hit it in the really long rough, you're still better to just pitch it back into play with an 8-iron or a wedge, but if you're just in the short rough, hybrids are the answer."

"Sold," Cheech said.

"I think this will come in handy in the Challenge Cup," Max said to him as they headed back toward the pro shop. "We're going to tighten up the fairways a little bit for the tournament."

The Challenge Cup was just over a week away. Cheech had submitted his scores and easily qualified for the team, but he was starting to get a little nervous about the event.

"How's the team looking this year?" Cheech asked.

"The ladies team is solid, but the guys will be in tough. With Glen's death last year and Stryker now playing for Blackhawk Ridge, we'll be counting on you, Ray and Bruce to play well if we're going to pull out a win."

"We'll give it our best shot," Cheech said.

Max knew they would. He just hoped their best was good enough.

CHAPTER 22: FOREPLAY

The Challenge Cup was always held on the September long weekend. On Saturday, the competition consisted of three best-ball matches for the men and three best-ball matches for the ladies. On Sunday, the pairings consisted of six alternate shot competitions, with a man and a woman on each team. On the holiday Monday, the event finished with twelve singles matches. Twenty-four points were available in total. If a match was tied, then each team earned a half-point. Since Blackhawk Ridge was the defending champion, they only needed twelve points to retain the cup. Riverview had to beat them outright to wrestle the cup away from them.

Every year, a reception was held at the club on the Friday night before the competition began. Since the Challenge Cup was a charity event, there were numerous activities held to raise money. Local companies and suppliers donated merchandise for a silent auction and a few items were raffled off through ticket sales. The club also donated the profits from liquor sales, so the event had the potential to raise a fair bit of money.

The designated charity had changed a few times since its inception. For the first few years, it had been the United Way, then it was the Heart and Stroke Foundation. This year it was Autism Canada. Max had created a brief video showing Tyler's golfing ability and the club had taken up the cause. As an added bonus, the great golfer Ernie Els, whose son Ben is autistic, had donated a golf bag with his signature on it as one of the auction items.

The reception was also when the team members for both teams were introduced and the matches for the first day of competition were announced. Max made a brief speech in tribute to Glen Watkins, their captain from the previous year, and then asked for a moment of silence in his memory. There were several tears shed when the Riverview team members donned golf caps with *"In Memory of Glen Watkins"* written on them.

"It seems strange seeing Stryker playing for Blackhawk Ridge," Bruce whispered to Ray as they stood at the front of the room with all of their teammates.

Ray scanned the faces of their opposition who stood on the other side of the podium. "Is that your son over there?"

"Sure is," Bruce replied. "Josh made their team. So did his girlfriend, Robyn. She's the one wearing the blue top."

All of the players from the Blackhawk team looked young and fit. Stryker was the oldest player on their team by far, but Ray knew he was probably their best player. "Could be another tough year," Ray whispered.

Max stepped up to the podium. "We're now going to announce the matches for tomorrow which will be a two-person best-ball. Since Blackhawk Ridge are the visitors this year, they get to go first."

Darren Fletcher, the pro from BlackHawk Ridge, moved toward the microphone. "First out on our side will be our two rookies, Josh Thompson and Kyle Smith."

Max called his team together in a huddle. "So who wants to be first out and take these guys on?" he whispered to the team.

"I'll go in the first group," Bruce said. "Josh has never beaten the old man in a match."

His wife, Marilyn, shot him a dirty look. She was a good golfer and had made the team, but she was more interested in everyone getting along than in winning. "I don't think it's a good idea for one family member to play another."

The final decision was up to Max. He thought for a second. He didn't want to start a family feud right out of the starting gate. "How about we put Cheech and Ray out in the first match? You guys play together all the time so I think you'll be a good pairing." He waited for their reaction.

"Sounds good to me," Cheech said.

Ray nodded his agreement.

"Okay, we'll send you guys out first. Bruce, I'll put you and George in our second group."

Bruce really wanted to go up against his son, but he relented. "I'll play wherever you think best."

Max stepped up to the podium. "Our first pairing will be Cheech Martin and Ray Ferguson."

The MC wrote the names of the first match on a huge whiteboard at the front of the room. The Riverview team got to go first in announcing their players for the second match.

"Our second group will be Bruce Thompson and George Wilson," Max said into the microphone.

Darren briefly huddled his team together to discuss who would be going up against them.

"Our second pairing will be Jeff Stryker and Brandon Young."

Bruce didn't know anything about the other fellow, but he knew he'd be in tough going up against Stryker. He hoped he didn't let the team down.

They continued to announce the names of the rest of the matches and the MC recorded them on the whiteboard.

"First match tees off tomorrow morning at ten. Good luck everyone."

There was a brief applause from the crowd.

"We're going to take a ten minute break for everyone to refresh their drinks," the MC said, "and then we'll be holding the auction and draws for the prizes. Last chance to get your tickets or your bids in."

* * *

As Cheech approached the bar, he saw Maggie standing in line. He hadn't spoken to her since she'd driven him home from the hospital several weeks ago. He debated turning in the other direction, but then realized it seemed stupid. He knew she was on the Blackhawk team; she knew he was playing for Riverview. It was inevitable they'd cross paths at some point over the weekend. Might as well get it over with.

"Good luck in your match tomorrow," Cheech said.

"Thanks," Maggie said. "You, too."

A few awkward seconds passed. She seemed to be studying his hair.

"I see you stopped using that crap in your hair."

"Yeah, I wasn't sure it was actually doing anything."

"I don't know why you started using it in the first

place. You look pretty good with some grey."

A few more awkward seconds passed.

"I heard you landed a position with NBT. Congratulations," Maggie said.

"Thanks. I like it there. How'd you know about it?"

"You know, people talk."

Maggie reached the front of the line. "Bacardi 1873 and coke," she said to the bartender.

"Make it two," Cheech said. He waved a twenty at the bartender. "I've got this."

"Thanks," Maggie said. "I thought you started drinking those new fruity shooter-like concoctions."

"Yeah, I did for a while, but I grew tired of them. I decided to go back to one of my old favourites."

She smiled at him. "I've heard that happens sometimes." She touched his hand. "Thanks for the drink. I've got to get back to my teammates."

* * *

It took about an hour to hold the raffles and announce the winners of the silent auction items.

"All right everyone," the MC said, "we're now ready to auction off the main prize for the evening. This one wasn't included in the items for the silent auction. We figured we'd raise more money by having live bidding for this very prestigious item."

He reached down and picked up the golf bag donated by Ernie Els and held it up so everyone could see it.

"This is a replica of the bag used by Ernie Els in the President's Cup competition. Not only has it been signed by Ernie Els, but it's also been signed by all of the members of the International Team. I see Jason Day's signature, Adam Scott's, and Canada's own Graham DeLaet. How about we start the bidding at five hundred dollars."

Numerous hands shot up and people started shouting out their bids. It quickly rose to over a thousand dollars.

"Twelve hundred," Bruce shouted as he raised his hand.

Two more bids followed quickly.

"Fifteen hundred," Josh said. He smiled at his father when he said it.

"Sixteen hundred," Bruce shouted.

Marilyn elbowed him in the ribs. "What are you doing bidding against Josh? That's his favourite golfer. Just let him have it."

Someone else bid seventeen hundred, but Josh quickly responded with eighteen hundred.

"Two thousand," Bruce shouted.

He leaned over to whisper to his wife. "I'm actually trying to buy it for Josh to give to him as a present. I didn't think he'd go this high."

"Twenty-one hundred," Josh yelled.

Marilyn shook her head. "You two are so damn competitive. You don't even realize what you're doing, do you?"

"Twenty-five hundred," Bruce shouted.

Bruce saw his son's shoulders slump. Josh waved his hand to the MC to indicate he was done bidding.

"Sold," the MC said.

CHAPTER 23: INTEGRITY OF THE GAME

The following morning, a small crowd gathered around the first tee to watch the players tee off. Even though Bruce was in the second match, he made sure he got there in time to see his son tee off in the first group. He could tell Josh was nervous with everyone watching and was pleased when he hit a good tee shot. His partner, Kyle, wasn't as fortunate and hit it in the bunker. Both Cheech and Ray found the fairway with their shots.

On the first day of competition, each player played their own ball. The team score on each hole was the lower of the scores of the teammates, or "best ball" as it was sometimes called.

"Good luck, son," Bruce said as Josh walked off the first tee.

Josh either didn't hear him, or pretended not to hear him. Bruce hadn't managed to talk with his son after their bidding war over the Ernie Els golf bag the night before. He had tried to call him, but it went straight to voice-mail. Marilyn hadn't said two words to him the rest of the night.

Bruce tried to turn his focus to his own match, but it didn't work. He found himself looking ahead wondering how his son's match was going rather than concentrating on his own. By the time they reached the sixth tee, they were already down by four to Stryker and his partner. George Wilson, Bruce's partner, was playing quite well. Bruce was the problem. He'd made five straight bogies and hadn't contributed anything to the team effort. To make matters worse, Stryker had birdied the second, third and fifth holes.

* * *

Up ahead in the first match, Cheech and Ray were having their own problems. Cheech's head wasn't in the game either. He was thinking about Maggie and their encounter the night before. He felt like they'd "*shared a moment*", but he wasn't entirely sure. His judgement, or more correctly, his lack thereof, had gotten him into all kinds of trouble over the last year. But he couldn't get her off his mind.

Cheech saw Max sitting in a golf cart up by the seventh green. As captain, Max had been there at the first tee to watch all the groups tee off. He was now making the rounds to get updates from the team.

"How's your match going?" Max asked.

"We're two down," Cheech replied. "Bruce's kid is killing us. He made a twenty-footer on the first hole for a birdie and just rolled in a thirty-footer for another on six. Ray is playing well, but I haven't contributed anything so far."

"Keep plugging away," Max said. "Getting the first point of the day is important, so let's see if you guys can turn this thing around."

"How are the other matches going?"

"Too early to tell," Max said. "Most have only played a few holes."

* * *

Max drove his golf cart over to the fourth hole to check on that match. He had lied to Cheech. This was becoming his worst nightmare. They were losing all three of the men's matches and one of the ladies matches. Another was all square. The only match they were ahead in was the last match of the day and they'd only played one hole so far.

Maybe Darren was right. Maybe they *were* too old to compete against the team from Blackhawk Ridge. This was shaping up to be another lopsided win for them.

Max knew his primary role as captain was to get the best out of his team. That's why he hadn't told Cheech how bad things were going. Every player had to believe they could win their match and that they were key to pulling out a victory. Sometimes, this meant he had to be a cheerleader. Other times, he had to be a calm advisor on strategy. And sometimes it meant he had to give someone a kick in the butt and tell them they simply had to do better. He wished he knew what to do.

At the end of the first day, Riverview was down four points to two. That was actually much better than it had looked all day. They lost all three of the men's matches so were down three-nil at one point. But the ladies had saved them from complete embarrassment by winning two out of their three matches, one of them by sinking a long putt on the eighteenth hole.

* * *

That evening, both teams met in the clubhouse to determine the matches for the next day. There was no ceremony this time like there had been on Friday night. This time, the captains sat down with their teams and Max and Darren slid pieces of paper across the table to each other as the draw was made.

The second day of competition consisted of a man and a woman on each team in an alternate-shot format. That meant that team members must trust each other and work well together, because your shot directly affected your partner's next shot. You might hit your shot onto the green giving your partner a good shot at birdie, or bury your shot in the bunker leaving an almost impossible up-and-down. This was the ultimate test of being a team player and many golfers struggled with this format.

Max met privately with his team before the draw. "Okay, I think we're going to have change things up a bit if we're going to turn things around in the competition. Stryker killed us today, winning his match seven-up with six to play. We need someone who's not afraid to go up against him."

"I'm willing to take him on," Cheech said.

"Who do you want as your partner?" Max asked.

"Doesn't matter. All of the ladies played well today."

"Thanks," Max said. "That makes it easier. I'm pretty sure Darren's going to send out Stryker in the last group tomorrow, so I'll hold you back to go out against him."

Max looked at Bruce. "The other player that destroyed us today was Josh. Bruce, you said you wanted to go up against him. You still want to do that?"

"Absolutely," Bruce said.

"I still don't think it's a good idea for one family member to play another," Marilyn said.

"Yeah, I know," Max said. "That's why I didn't put them up against each other in the first round, but we need the point and Bruce thinks he can beat him."

Marilyn pursed her lips. "Well then don't pair me up with Bruce, because there's no way I'm competing against my own son."

He had no intention of making Bruce and Marilyn partners. Some couples play well together in competition and others don't. He knew there was already plenty of tension between them.

Max headed into the meeting room where Darren, the captain of the Blackhawk Ridge team, was waiting. Darren slid the piece of paper with his first pairing over to Max.

"We're sending the team of Josh Thompson and Robyn Baker out first," Darren said.

Max was expecting this. "We're going with Bruce Thompson and Ally Walker."

This seemed to catch Darren by surprise. "Interesting. The father-son competition should lead to some lively discussion at the next family gathering."

Max and Darren continued to exchange the names of their team members for the matches the next day.

"For my last pairing of the day, I'm going with the team of Cheech Martin and Anne-Marie Tremblay," Max said.

Darren only had two names left. "Jeff Stryker and Maggie Martin."

The colour drained from Max's face. He had deliberately held Cheech's name to the end because he wanted him to go up against Stryker. But he hadn't even thought about who Stryker's partner would be. He wondered how Cheech would feel going up against his ex.

* * *

For matches on day two of the competition, it had already been decided that they'd go with a back nine start, which meant that groups would start on the tenth hole rather than the first. Some players found the front nine easier, others preferred the back nine. Since most matches were decided early before playing the whole eighteen holes, this helped ensure that all players would have to play each hole on the course at least once during the competition.

"Good luck, son," Bruce said as he put his hand out.

Josh shook his hand, but didn't say anything. He had his game face on.

"Play well, Robyn," Bruce said.

"You too, sir," Robyn replied.

Ally, Bruce's playing partner, also shook hands with Josh and Robyn.

Since today's competition was an alternate shot format, it had been decided that all holes would be played from the white tees. This made the course play a little longer than most of the ladies were used to and a little shorter than normal for the men.

It also introduced the first strategic decision for each team, whether to have the male partner tee off on the even numbered holes and the female partner tee off on the odd numbered holes, or vice versa.

Josh hit first, deciding to try to cut the corner on the dogleg. He pounded his drive and almost drove the green, leaving Robyn an easy chip shot. He beamed as he picked up his tee.

Bruce waved for Ally to hit the tee shot for their team. He knew that Josh could easily out-drive him by twenty yards and didn't want to give him the psychological advantage of going head-to-head with him off the tee. Ally hit a good drive, but she left Bruce with a second shot of about a hundred and fifty yards. He hit a pretty good approach into the green, leaving a twenty-five foot putt.

"Nice drive, son," Bruce said when they reached Josh's ball. "You must have hit that over two seventy."

Robyn was left with a very short pitch shot and hit it about three feet past the hole. It looked like they were going to take the early lead in the match.

Everyone was surprised when Ally rolled in her long putt for birdie. Suddenly, the three-footer facing Josh looked a lot more ominous. Now he had to make it just to tie the hole.

Bruce watched as Josh lined up his putt. He sincerely hoped he'd make it. It looked like Josh hit a good putt, but it lipped out and hung on the edge of the hole.

"Tough break, Josh," Bruce said. "You were robbed."

That one missed putt caused Josh to lose all confidence. He didn't make a putt of any significant length for the rest of the day.

Bruce found it painful to watch. Someone once said that *"golf is eighty percent mental, and the rest is all in your head."* Josh had become the poster boy for that saying.

Bruce and Ally won the match five-up with only four holes left to play.

* * *

In the last match of the day, Cheech and Anne-Marie were in a close match with Maggie and Stryker. Neither team had taken more than a one-up lead through the entire day.

Cheech thought it would feel strange playing against his ex, but there was surprisingly little tension between them. In fact, Cheech admired how Maggie was holding up. He knew she was a good golfer; there was never any doubt about that. He liked how she carried herself, particularly with Stryker.

It was becoming obvious that Stryker was a bit of a control freak, always wanting things done a certain way – his way. But Maggie was standing up to him. There were a few times during the match when Stryker tried to tell her how to hit a certain shot, like the time she was faced with hitting it out of a thick lie in the rough.

"Just wedge it back into the fairway," Stryker said. "That's the smart shot. I'll hit the next one onto the green and we'll see if we can salvage a par."

"The lie is not that bad," Maggie said. "I'm pretty sure I can get it on the green with my hybrid."

Stryker took another look at the lie. "Don't think so. Just hit the wedge."

Cheech watched as Maggie took the head cover off her hybrid.

"I think this is a mistake," Stryker warned.

Cheech wanted to jump in to defend her, wanted to tell Stryker to zip his pie-hole, but it wasn't his place. He wasn't her partner, not in this match, not in anything.

Maggie hit the hybrid and the ball flew out of the rough, landed just short of the green, but bounced up to within a few feet of the hole.

"We got lucky there," Stryker said.

Maggie didn't say a word, just quietly put the head cover back on and slid the club back into her bag.

Cheech smiled, looked over at Maggie, and discretely tipped his hat.

She smiled back.

Even though that shot caused them to lose the hole, Cheech didn't seem to mind.

As they came up to the last hole, Cheech and Anne-Marie were one-down.

"We really need you to win this hole," Max said to Cheech before he hit his tee shot. He stressed how important it was for them to win the last hole to salvage a tie in the match.

Since it had been a back-nine start, the final hole of the match was the ninth hole, a long par-five that finished in front of the clubhouse. With the other matches already completed, all of the other competitors were gathered behind the green to watch the last match of the day.

Cheech hit a perfect tee shot, easily clearing the bunker down the right side of the fairway. Stryker's shot was almost a duplicate copy, but finished just a couple of yards behind.

Maggie hit her second shot up between the two fairway bunkers, in perfect position for an approach into the green. However, Anne-Marie was feeling the pressure of the moment. She blocked her shot to the right and it flew into a small grove of pine trees in the right rough.

"I'm so sorry," she said.

"Don't worry about it," Cheech said. "Maybe we'll catch a break."

They watched as Stryker hit his third shot onto the green, leaving a birdie putt of about ten feet. Cheech knew their chances of winning the last hole were practically nil.

As they walked toward the trees, Cheech was hoping their ball had hit one of the trees and bounced back into the rough. It wouldn't be an easy shot, but it would at least give them a chance. They all searched the rough, but didn't see it.

"I think I see one right in the middle of the trees," Maggie said. She pointed to it.

"We're screwed," Cheech thought to himself. He pushed the branches aside as he maneuvered his way inside. He peered down at the ball.

"Yep, this is our ball," he said.

He was surprised at how open it was in the middle of the grove of trees. Although there were thick branches on the outside of the grove, there were hardly any branches on the inside. He realized he might have enough room to make a swing.

Anne-Marie had already assumed they were going to have to declare the ball unplayable and take a penalty drop.

"Where do you think we should drop it?" she asked.

"We might not have to," Cheech said. "I might have a shot. Hand me my eight-iron."

Anne-Marie passed the club to him through the branches.

As Cheech surveyed his options, he realized he could see the pin through a gap in the branches. If he could make good contact with the ball and hit it through that gap, he might actually be able to get the ball on the green.

Stryker peered through the trees to assess the situation. "He's got nothing," he whispered to Maggie.

Maggie looked between the branches to do her own assessment. She could see the shot that Cheech was going to try to play. "I wouldn't be so sure," she said.

"Have an eye," Cheech shouted. "This could go anywhere."

He gripped his eight-iron and tried to visualize the ball flying through the gap in the branches. He took his stance, but then realized his right foot was on top of a pine cone. He kicked it away with his foot and then twisted his feet down into the pine needles to get a better stance.

When he did this, a dead branch that was lying underneath the pine needles twisted. It extended up close to where the ball was sitting. Cheech saw the ball move, only about an inch or so, but it definitely moved.

"Shit!" he said.

"What happened?" Anne-Marie asked. "Did you hit it? I didn't see it come out."

He moved the ball back to where it was initially and then took a swing, mostly out of anger at himself. The ball sailed through the gap in the branches and bounded up onto the green.

"Nice shot," Anne-Marie shouted.

As Cheech pushed the branches aside and came out from the trees, he looked at Anne-Marie, Maggie and Stryker.

"We have to take a penalty shot," Cheech announced.

"Why?" Anne-Marie asked. "You hit it up on the green."

"The ball moved when I was taking my stance."

Stryker knew the rule. "Are you sure you caused it to move?"

Cheech sighed. "Yeah, I'm sure. I moved the ball back to where it was and then hit it, so we have to take a one-shot penalty. We're lying four up on the green."

When Maggie and Stryker two-putted for a par five, Cheech removed his hat, held out his hand and conceded the match. Even if they made their putt, the best they could do was a five. Since Stryker and Maggie were one-up coming into the last hole, they'd won the match.

Max came over to congratulate the winners as well. "That was a hell of a match," he said.

"Sorry I let you down," Cheech said.

"You didn't let me down at all," Max said. "You showed a lot of integrity calling that penalty on yourself. Not a lot of people would have done that."

"Yeah, but I got careless and let the team down."

"You did nothing of the sort. We win as a team and lose as a team. And we've got one more day to go."

CHAPTER 24: THE S-WORD

Later that evening, both teams gathered in the clubhouse to determine the pairings for the last day of the competition. The teams had split the matches that day in the alternate shot format, but Riverview still trailed seven points to five overall after the second day of competition. There were twelve points up for grabs in Monday's singles matches.

The ladies matches were scheduled to go off first the next day, which suited Max just fine. The ladies from Riverview had managed to win more points than the men so far. He hoped the ladies would continue to play well and win four out of six of their matches to tie up the competition.

As expected, Darren was sending out Stryker in the anchor spot on the last day and Max had countered with Cheech. Although Cheech had lost earlier that day, Max was pleased with how Cheech had handled the pressure.

Max put Bruce up against his son again in the second last match of the day. Marilyn had once again voiced her opposition.

* * *

As Bruce and Marilyn left the clubhouse that evening, they saw Josh out on the putting green. There was barely enough light to see, but Josh continued to hit putt after putt. He was obviously upset about his play that day.

"You should go talk to him," Marilyn said.

"Yeah, I know," Bruce said, "but I don't know what to say."

They walked to their car in the parking lot.

"You wait here," Bruce said when they got there. "I have an idea."

He opened the trunk and pulled out the Ernie Els signature golf bag. He headed back over to the putting green. Josh seemed locked in on trying to fix his putting woes and didn't notice him approach.

"Tough day out there today," Bruce said.

Josh looked up. "Hi Dad. Yeah, it was."

"Have you figured out what the problem is?"

Josh sighed. "Haven't a clue. I seem to be okay here on the putting green, but it all falls apart when I'm out on the course."

Josh noticed what his father was carrying. "What's with the bag?"

"It's actually for you."

Bruce placed the bag in front of him.

"I don't understand," Josh said. "You out-bid me for it. You won it fair and square."

"I was trying to get it for *you*. I was planning to hang onto it and give it to you next Christmas. I'll have you know, you made me pay about five hundred bucks more than I wanted to. I thought you were never going to stop bidding."

"Sorry. Why didn't you say something?"

"I didn't know you were going to bid on it and then things just started to snowball from there. I was hoping it would be a surprise."

Josh hit another putt. "So why are you giving it to me now?"

"Cause you look like you need it. Besides, I wasn't sure you'd be talking to me after I kick your ass in our match tomorrow."

Josh smiled. "Bring it on, old man."

* * *

When Cheech left the clubhouse that evening, he was surprised to see Maggie leaning up against his car.

"Maggie, what are you doing here?"

"Waiting for you. I just wanted to let you know that I was pretty impressed with you calling that penalty on yourself today. It probably cost you the match."

"Maybe, maybe not," Cheech said. "I really didn't have a choice."

"Sure you did. You're the only person in the world who knew that ball moved. We'd be none the wiser if you hadn't told us."

"Yeah, but *I'd* know."

Maggie studied his face. "I don't understand how a man can have so much integrity about a stupid golf game and yet have absolutely none when it comes to cheating on his wife."

Cheech looked around to make sure there was no one else in the parking lot. "Not that it makes any difference at this point, but I never actually cheated on you."

"Oh, come on. I'm not stupid. What about chicky at the convention or your little running mate that I met at the hospital?"

"Look, I know you don't believe me, but I've never

slept with anyone else."

Maggie studied his face. He looked like he was telling the truth, but she couldn't be sure. She didn't want to be played for a fool. "Well, it wasn't for lack of trying."

Cheech leaned up against the car and stared up into the darkening sky. "You're probably right there, but I'm still not sure if I could have actually gone through with it."

Maggie crossed her arms in front of her chest. "Then why do it?"

"Because it felt good to know that someone young and attractive was interested in an old fart like me. It had been a long time since anyone had."

"What about me?"

"You don't count. You're my wife."

"I don't count? Well, *that* says a lot right there."

Cheech reached out and touched her arm. "That's not what I meant. Of course you count, but I mean it's nice to know that someone other than your spouse finds you attractive."

"Well, welcome to the club buddy. Most days, I don't think I could turn a man's head even if my hair was on fire."

Cheech looked at her. "You still turn lots of heads. I see it all the time."

Nothing was said for several seconds.

"So, you never actually cheated on me?" Maggie asked. "You promise?"

"Never. I promise."

They both continued to lean up against the car staring into the darkening sky for several minutes.

"So what do we do now?" Cheech asked.

"I don't know," Maggie said. She looked around the parking lot. "I don't suppose you can give me a ride over to Blackhawk Ridge, could you? I left my car there and I think my ride has already left."

"Sure," Cheech said. He hit the button on his keys to unlock the doors.

Maggie walked around to the passenger side of the car. "How the hell do you fit into this thing?" she asked. "I feel like my ass is going to be dragging on the ground."

"Yeah, this wasn't one of my smartest purchases," Cheech said. "It's too small. My clubs barely fit in the trunk. I'm thinking about trading it in and getting something more practical."

Cheech started the car and slowly drove the car out of the parking lot and through the gated community. When he reached the main road, he accelerated, quickly shifting gears as he drove the twisting road through the hills toward Blackhawk Ridge.

"It looks like it's a fun car to drive," Maggie said.

"It is," Cheech said. He looked over at her. "Want to give it a try?"

"I would, but I don't know how to drive a standard."

"It's not that hard. I'll teach you."

Cheech pulled the car over to the shoulder and they traded seats.

"It's not in gear right now," Cheech said. "First gear is up and to the left, second gear is straight back down, third is back up and to the right, and fourth is back down. We won't worry about fifth gear or reverse at this point. Just push in the clutch when you're switching gears and then give it some gas and slowly let it out until it catches."

Maggie looked in the mirror to check to make sure that no other cars were coming, revved the engine a little bit, put it in first gear and then released the clutch. The car lurched forward and then stalled.

"Shit. Are you sure you want me to do this? I don't

want to wreck your car."

"Don't worry about it," Cheech said. "Give it another try. This time, try to release the clutch a little slower while at the same time giving it a bit more gas."

Maggie gave it another try and successfully got it moving forward this time. She accelerated as she pulled off the shoulder and onto the road.

"Great," Cheech said. "Now push in the clutch and shift into second."

Maggie tried, but the stick shift wouldn't slide all of the way down. She pulled a little harder and released the clutch. There was a horrible grinding sound, but it seemed to finally make it into second gear.

"That didn't sound good," Maggie said.

"You're fine, just keep going."

Maggie continued to accelerate and shifted into third gear, this time more smoothly. "I think I'm getting the hang of it."

She stayed in third gear while she navigated her way along the twisting road. "You're right, this *is* a fun car to drive."

In her rear view mirror, she saw a car coming up behind her. "Uh, oh. Someone's behind me."

"You're fine," Cheech reassured her. "He'll just pass you if you're going too slow."

But Maggie knew the road had too many curves for them to pass and she felt too nervous with someone right behind her. At the next turn in the road, she pulled off the main road and down a gravel side road.

"Shift her back down into second," Cheech said.

It took a few attempts, but Maggie eventually managed to get it into second gear. She continued along the gravel road looking for a place to turn around, but none appeared. Eventually, the road came to a dead end and they parked in a clearing that overlooked the city. There was a small sign that said they were at "Blackhawk Lookout."

From the ridge, they could see the glow of the city below them. They could also see the lights from the clubhouse at Riverview.

"It's pretty," Maggie said.

Cheech looked around. There was another car parked at the far end of the clearing. He didn't see anyone in it, but the windows seemed to be fogged up.

"Uh, oh," he said.

"What?" Maggie asked.

"We seem to have ended up in a make-out spot."

"Really? How do you know that?"

Cheech nodded his head toward the car at the far end of the clearing.

"So, is this where you bring all your dates in your hot little sports car?" Maggie asked.

"Don't blame me. You were the one driving. Besides, I don't think this car is big enough to make out in."

Maggie looked around. It *was* a pretty small car. It had a back seat, but it didn't look big enough for a person to actually sit in. The only thing on it was Cheech's jacket.

"Oh, I don't know," Maggie said. "Where there's a will, there's a way. Do the seats recline?"

Cheech reached down and pressed the power seat adjuster. His seat-back gradually moved back until it was almost fully reclined.

"How'd you do that?" Maggie asked.

"Just hit the button on the side of your seat."

Maggie did and her seat fully reclined. They stared at each other for a few seconds, both seemingly wondering what was going to happen next.

"I've missed you," Cheech said.

"I've missed you too," Maggie replied. She raised an eyebrow. "You know, it would be a shame for you to trade this car in before it had been properly christened. If you slide your left leg over onto my seat and angle yourself a bit sideways, this might work."

Cheech did as he was told. Then Maggie swung her leg over so she was straddling him. When she lifted her head up to remove her top, she accidently hit the button that controlled the moon roof and it slid open.

"Sorry about that," she said as she nestled back down toward him. She felt something hard underneath her.

"Oh Cheech, you really *did* miss me."

Cheech groaned. "That's not me. That's the gear shift!"

Maggie giggled like a teenager. Cheech laughed until he snorted.

Suddenly their car lit up. Another car was driving through the clearing and its headlights shone directly at their sports car.

Maggie poked her head out of the moon roof. "Shit, it's the cops!"

The policeman didn't get out of his car, probably not wanting to embarrass anyone. He slowly continued driving through the clearing toward the other car and then circled back toward them. "The lookout closes at dusk," he announced over his loudspeaker, "so let's move along."

Maggie scrambled to put her top back on. Cheech shimmied out the passenger door from underneath her and felt his back twinge when he did so. He slowly walked around the car to the driver's side.

"Good evening, officer," Cheech said. "We'll be on our way shortly."

The officer lowered his window and shone his flashlight at Cheech. "I don't suppose you have anyone in there with you who could be under age," the officer said.

Maggie got out of the car and the officer directed the flashlight at her. "Thanks for the compliment, officer, but I can assure you that I'm old enough to be doing this type of thing."

The officer just shook his head and turned off the flashlight.

* * *

The next morning, Cheech was on the driving range warming up before his match against Stryker. He was just going through the motions as his mind was on what had happened the night before.

After his rendezvous with Maggie had been interrupted by the police officer, cooler heads had prevailed. He had simply driven Maggie back to her car at Blackhawk Ridge. Fortunately, it was just a short distance from the lookout, as no words were exchanged between them on the drive. He had thought about asking her back to his place, but didn't for some reason. He wondered if she had wanted him to.

When she got out of the car, all he had said was "Good luck in your match tomorrow". *What a lame thing to say.* She had looked at him with a puzzled look on her face and then left without saying a word.

Cheech hit another practice shot. He knew she would be over on the first tee, as her match would be starting soon. He should probably go over to talk to her, but he still had no idea as to what he would say.

When Cheech hit his next shot, he felt his back twinge a bit. The ball hit the hosel of the club and careened wildly to the right.

Bruce, who was warming up on the range beside him, turned to look at him. "Did you just shank that?"

Suddenly, everyone else on the range stopped and turned toward them. Bruce had dared to say the S-word out loud. The shanks were every golfer's worst nightmare. When a golfer has the shanks, even his closest friends will abandon him like he has the worst contagious disease possible.

"No," Cheech lied. "My back is a little stiff this morning. I just hit it off the toe."

He tried to stretch out his back. He was sure he had tweaked it while trying one of their acrobatic maneuvers in the car last night. There was no way he was going to share that information with anyone.

He hit a few more warmup shots that went long and straight.

The first match of the day was now teeing off. "Now on the tee, representing Blackhawk Ridge, Maggie Martin," the loudspeaker announced.

On the practice tee, Cheech clanked another one and it squirreled to the right, bouncing in front of the other players on the range. There was no denying it this time. A shank has a very distinctive sound.

No one said a word, but the range was cleared within seconds. No one wanted to be around him.

Cheech was alone and in trouble. Was the glitch in his swing being caused by his twitchy back? Or was the problem in his head? He didn't have a clue.

CHAPTER 25: THUNDER & LIGHTNING

Max was late getting to the golf course that morning. This, the final day of the Challenge Cup, was the one morning he didn't want to be late. But Sylvia, his father's homecare assistant, hadn't shown up. After numerous unanswered phone calls, Max had finally clued in that she wouldn't be coming at all. It was a holiday, Labour Day Monday, and she wasn't supposed to work.

Max had called his sister to see if she could take care of their father for the day, but she hadn't answered either. So here was Max, driving like a mad man with his father, Arthur, in the passenger seat beside him, trying to get to the golf course before the first match of the day teed off.

"Where are we?" Arthur asked when they pulled into the parking lot.

"Riverview," Max said.

"What are we doing here?"

Max had already explained the situation to his father several times that morning, but it didn't seem to be sinking in. His confusion and forgetfulness seemed to be getting worse and worse with each passing day.

"Dad, I don't have time for this," Max pleaded. "Please just stay in the golf cart. I've got a lot to do today."

Max had planned to meet with his team before the first match teed off to deliver some kind of inspirational speech, but the first group was already on the second hole by the time they arrived. Probably just as well. Panic was not something a team should see in their captain before they hit their first shot.

Riverview was starting the last day of the competition two points behind. Max arrived at the first tee as the third match of the day was about to tee off. Maggie Martin, from Blackhawk Ridge, was going up against Riverview's Anne-Marie Tremblay. Maggie pushed her tee shot into the right rough, but Anne-Marie striped hers right down the middle of the fairway.

"Looks like these ladies don't really need any help from you," Arthur said.

Max sighed and looked at his father. But he was probably right. At this point, it was really up to the players themselves to pull out a win.

Max headed out to the second green to see how the first match was going. Marilyn Thompson, Bruce's wife, was representing Riverview in the first match and going up against Janice Smith. Psychologically, it was important that Marilyn win the first match to pull Riverview back to within a point. Falling three points behind Blackhawk Ridge might prove too big of a hurdle to overcome.

Max saw both ladies hit their approaches into the green. Janice had about a twenty foot putt, with Marilyn's birdie putt about half that distance. Both ladies were smiling and chatting while they played. *Don't they realize how important this first match is?*

Janice hit her birdie putt about three feet by the hole.

"That's good," Marilyn said, conceding the next shot.

Max grimaced. *She shouldn't be conceding that putt. God, that woman doesn't have a competitive bone in her body!*

Marilyn missed her birdie putt as well and both women headed for the third tee, continuing to chat up a storm.

Max wanted to go talk to Marilyn to tell her to stop conceding such long putts, but then reconsidered. He knew Marilyn wasn't happy with him for asking Bruce to go up against his son in the matches. She'd probably start conceding even longer putts just to spite him. He decided to turn his focus to the other matches.

In the second ladies match, Ally Walker was going up against Becky Henderson. Becky was one of the top golfers in the city, so it would be hard for Ally to win that match for Riverview. But as the match progressed, Ally was putting up quite a fight.

Max and his father followed that group for most of the day. Arthur seemed bored, but Max was thankful that he seemed content to just sit in the cart. Max was fully engaged, continually giving Ally encouragement and advice. He was even more despondent than she was when she lost the match by missing a short putt on the seventeenth hole.

After that match ended, Max raced up to the eighteenth green to see how Marilyn's match would end up. It appeared that the match was going down to the wire. He watched as Marilyn drained a long putt. *Was that the winning putt?* No, it couldn't be because Janice was lining up her putt. Janice ran her putt three feet by once again.

"That's good," Marilyn said.

Had Marilyn just conceded a three-footer to win the match? Or was that for the tie? Max was beside himself not knowing what was going on. He tried to remain calm as both ladies shook hands and walked off the green toward him. They continued to chat like they didn't have a care in the world.

"How'd you ladies do?" Max asked.

"Oh, Marilyn won the match five holes ago," Janice said. "We just played out the round for fun."

Marilyn put her hand on Max's shoulder. "It's just killing you, isn't it? Imagine, playing the game just for fun."

* * *

Max was relieved when the results of the ladies matches were posted. Riverview had managed to win four out of the six ladies matches and had put the overall competition into a tie with nine points each. There were six more points available in the men's matches. But a tie in the men's matches wouldn't be good enough. If everything ended in a tie, Blackhawk Ridge would retain the cup as defending champions.

As Max headed over toward the first tee, he heard the distant rumble of thunder. Storm clouds were starting to gather.

* * *

Bruce stood on the first tee waiting for his son to arrive for their match. He knew Josh was there because he had seen him earlier on the range. He heard a trunk slam in the parking lot and looked over to see his son approaching, carrying his clubs in his new *Ernie Els Signature* golf bag.

"I figured this might bring me some luck today," Josh said when he arrived.

Bruce sensed the confidence in his son's stride. It

continued out on the golf course. Bruce was playing well, but Josh was playing better. If Bruce made a birdie putt, Josh would roll one in right after him. When they made the turn after nine holes, Josh was three up. It looked like Josh might actually beat his father for the first time.

The first crack in the armour didn't appear until the par-three twelfth hole. Josh hit his tee shot on the green and had about a ten foot putt for birdie. Bruce hit a terrible tee shot that barely cleared the water hazard. It hit the bank and the ball trickled back into the edge of the water.

In a regular game, Bruce would have simply taken a penalty shot, dropped another ball, and pitched it onto the green trying to salvage a bogey. But in match play, holes were simply won or lost. It didn't matter whether your competitor won the hole by one shot, or six. Bruce knew that Josh was going to make a par at worst.

"It's barely in the water," Bruce said. "I'm going to try to play it."

He took off his right shoe and sock, rolled up the right leg of his pants, and then put his foot in the water.

"Christ, it's cold!"

Bruce hovered his club above the water and then took a mighty swing. The ball came flying out of the water, landed on the green, took one bounce, hit the pin about a foot off the ground, and then fell straight down into the hole.

"Here we go again," Josh said.

Bruce hadn't even seen the ball go in. He was too busy trying to maintain his balance and not fall backwards into the water.

"What happened? Where did it go?"

Josh pulled the ball out of the hole. "You are such a lucky bastard!"

Josh missed his putt, so Bruce won the hole with a birdie. On the par-five thirteenth hole, Josh hit his tee shot into the water and had to take a penalty shot, so Bruce won that hole as well. They both made pars on the next hole, but Bruce birdied the fifteenth hole to square the match.

They heard the rumble of thunder behind them when they stood on the sixteenth tee. Bruce turned to see a huge storm approaching.

"I'm not sure we're going to finish before the storm hits," Bruce said.

* * *

One hole behind, in the last match of the day, Cheech was also trying to mount a comeback in his match against Stryker.

Since his performance on the driving range, Cheech had been worried about the shanks all day. Some people say the hardest shot in golf is the shot you're faced with after you've shanked one and Cheech was in full agreement. Rather than being aggressive and attacking the course, Cheech just felt relief whenever he hit the ball in the centre of the clubface.

Stryker was playing like a golfing machine, always playing the smart shot, always making solid contact. Stryker was three up in the match after the first nine holes. Cheech knew there were plenty of golf stories about triumphs and tragedies on the back nine, but he knew that Stryker was not going to wilt unless he started applying some pressure on him.

On the par-four dogleg tenth hole, Stryker hit an iron into the middle of the fairway, the smart and safe shot. Cheech pulled his driver and aimed just to the right of the houses that bordered the dogleg on the left. When he first hit it, he thought for sure he was going to end up in someone's back yard, but the wind slowly pushed it back on line. It landed just short of the green, but bounced forward leaving Cheech a thirty footer for eagle.

This seemed to rattle Stryker, but only for a second. He calmly hit his second shot onto the green and two-putted for par. When Cheech hit his eagle putt up to within a foot, Stryker conceded the birdie and the hole to Cheech.

"Pretty gutsy shot," Stryker said as they walked off the green. "You probably only make that shot two out of ten times."

"Yeah, I got lucky," Cheech said. He thought Stryker might have even over-estimated his chances of hitting the green with his tee shot.

They both birdied the par-five eleventh hole and parred the par-three twelfth, so Cheech was still two down as he stood on the thirteenth tee. The thirteenth hole is a long par-five that sweeps to the left with a large water hazard bordering the left side, all the way to the green. Cheech took an aggressive line aiming directly over the water. He smoked his tee shot, but there was still some doubt as to whether it would clear the water. He breathed a sigh of relief when the ball landed on dry land.

Stryker hit a three-wood to the middle of the fairway. On his second shot, he hit a three-iron leaving an easy wedge shot into the green.

The smart shot would have been for Cheech to hit his second shot to the right, avoiding any chance of going in the water. But what was the point of making a risky tee shot if he wasn't willing to go for it with his second shot as well? He pulled his three wood and aimed directly at the flag.

"See it, feel it, trust it," he thought to himself.

He hit it perfectly and the ball cleared the water landing on the green. He got lucky. He got even luckier when it looked like his ball was going to roll off the back of the green, but it circled and came back down the hill, stopping just four feet away from the hole.

No one was more surprised than Cheech when he saw Stryker chunk his approach shot into the water. He'd never seen Stryker hit such a poor shot.

"You win the hole," Stryker conceded.

Cheech was now only one down.

When they reached the fourteenth tee, Cheech noticed several people standing around the green watching. They were the golfers whose matches were already over. That must mean the overall winner still hadn't been decided.

Both Cheech and Stryker hit good shots onto the green and two-putted for par. As Cheech was walking to the next tee, Max pulled up in his golf cart.

"How's your match going?" Max asked.

"I'm one down," Cheech said. "How's the team doing?"

"It looks like it's going right down to the wire. We need you to pull this one out." Max gave him a fist pump before driving off.

The fifteenth hole is a long par-four with a challenging tee shot over water. Cheech had the honour and took the head cover off of his driver. He knew he had to continue to apply pressure to Stryker. If we was going to win the match, he was going to have to make birdies. He doubted Stryker would bogey any of the remaining holes.

Once again, he took an aggressive line over the water. He hit a perfect tee shot which easily cleared the water, leaving him an easy wedge into the green.

Stryker played the smart shot and hit the middle of the

fairway. He hit a seven iron on his next shot and found the middle of the green.

As Cheech stood over his second shot, he noticed that the crowd behind the green had grown. He could see Max and his father in the golf cart. All of the ladies matches were over so they were all gathered behind the green to see how everything would play out.

And that's when he saw Maggie. She was standing with her teammates from Blackhawk Ridge. He wondered if she had won her match. He wondered if she was cheering for her teammates, or hoping he would win. He wondered if she had thought about last night as much as he had.

Focus, dammit. Focus on the shot.

He was caught between deciding whether to hit his pitching wedge or his gap wedge. He could feel the adrenaline rushing through his body. *It's probably better to pound the gap wedge rather than take a little off the pitching wedge.* He didn't think he'd be able to hit any kind of finesse shot at this point.

He pulled the gap wedge and lined up the shot. He kept his head down and thought he had made a good swing, but the crowd gasped when they heard the sound, even before they saw where the ball ended up.

"He shanked it," someone from the crowd said.

The ball careened to the right, took three crazy bounces sending it even farther to the right, and ended up out of bounds.

Cheech just stood there, dumbfounded.

Behind him, there was another rumble of thunder. In the distance, there was a flash of lightning.

The horn sounded a few seconds later. That was the signal to get off the course. A golf course is the last place you want to be in a thunder storm.

As the rain started to fall, Cheech continued to just stand there looking at the club in his hand. It was like he had just thrown a hand grenade and he was left there holding the pin in his hand.

"Do you want a ride into the clubhouse or are you just going to wait there until you get hit by lightning?"

Cheech turned to see who it was.

It was Maggie.

CHAPTER 26: TOWARD THE LIGHT

Max sat in his office in the pro shop along with Darren, the captain of the team from Blackhawk Ridge.

"I'm not sure we're going to get this in," Darren said.

Max looked at the weather forecast that was displayed on his computer screen. "According to this, the storm is going to last another couple of hours, but then it's clear after that."

"It'll be almost dark by then," Darren said.

If this was the middle of the summer, they'd have several more hours of daylight. But now that it was September, the days were getting shorter.

"So we'll probably not be able to finish this until tomorrow," Max said.

"Our guys can't play tomorrow," Darren said. "I know all of your players are retired, but my guys have jobs. Stryker told me he's in court first thing tomorrow."

"So what do we do?" Max asked.

"Well, normally the matches would be scored however they stand when play is suspended. We were all tied up with three matches still on the course. Your guy, Ray

Ferguson, was one-up coming down eighteen. Bruce and Josh were all tied up heading to the seventeenth. And Stryker was two-up with three to play. So, doing the math, we'd end up tied with twelve points each."

Max knew that a tie meant that Blackhawk Ridge retained the cup. "Not acceptable," he said.

"The only other option is to declare all matches still out on the course a draw, but we still end up with the same result overall. Look, I know the win is important to you, but you have to be reasonable."

Max stared out the window. It was still raining hard.

"I think it might be starting to clear up."

* * *

All of the players went to the clubhouse during the rain delay. Players who had already completed their matches could relax and have a drink or two, but the players from the last three matches were a nervous bunch. They knew that it was up to them to decide who would win the Challenge Cup when, or if, play resumed. Ray and Bruce were sitting at a table by the window watching the storm.

"Think we'll be getting back out there?" Ray asked.

"It's not looking too promising," Bruce said. "Probably just as well for me. I'm lucky to be still tied in my match. Josh is playing really well."

"I hope we do," Ray said. "I'm one up, and I'd already hit a good tee shot on eighteen when the horn blew. I'm pretty sure I can make par from there so it'll take a birdie to beat me." Ray looked around the room. "Have you seen Cheech?"

"No, but I've heard people whispering that he shanked one on fifteen and he's two down with three to play. He's probably hiding somewhere. If it was me, that's what I'd be doing."

"Me too, but that's probably the last thing he needs. We should go find him."

Bruce nodded his agreement and they both headed off in search of their golfing buddy and teammate. They checked the pro shop, the men's locker room, even the pool area, but didn't find him.

* * *

Cheech and Maggie were still sitting in the golf cart. They'd driven the cart down the ramp into the cart storage area underneath the pro shop to get out of the rain. Maggie had tried to get him to head up to the clubhouse, but Cheech didn't feel like being around anyone in his current state of mind. Maggie decided to stay with him.

"It's just a game, you know," Maggie said.

That was about the third time she'd said it. In fact, she'd been doing all the talking. Cheech was just sitting in the cart with his cap pulled down over his eyes, not saying a word. The silence was deafening.

Cheech finally raised the peak of his hat up, just a bit. "Where do we stand?"

Maggie looked over at him. She knew he wasn't asking about the match. "I'm not sure."

"What about last night?"

"I wasn't thinking clearly last night," Maggie said. "I don't think you were either. I think we just got caught up in the, um, *heat* of the moment."

"So what do we do now?" Cheech asked.

Maggie thought for a few seconds. "How about we just take things slow and see how it all plays out?"

Cheech sat up a little straighter in his seat. "Are you saying you're going to give me another chance? That there's still hope for us?"

Maggie smiled. "You know what they say. It's not over 'til it's over."

* * *

A few hours later, Max pushed the button to give the horn two quick blasts. That was the signal to resume play. Although it was still raining a bit, the threat of a lightning strike had passed.

Because it was so late in the day and they were afraid of running out of daylight, both captains had agreed to forego any warmup time for their players. The three remaining matches headed back out onto the course.

Max jumped into his cart and headed out to the eighteenth hole with his father, Arthur, in the passenger seat beside him.

Ray did as he had predicted. He hit his second shot onto the green and had an easy two-putt for par. When his competitor missed his birdie putt, it meant that Ray won his match. Riverview was now one point ahead with two matches still on the course.

"We're going to run out of daylight before the other two matches finish," Max said to his father.

"Why don't you just light it up?" Arthur asked.

Max shook his head at his father. "This isn't a baseball stadium, Dad. You can't just turn on the lights like you're playing a double-header."

"No, but you can do what we did back in the '78 Invitational."

"What are you talking about?" Max asked.

"I can't believe you don't remember," Arthur said. "The 1978 Invitational in Ottawa. That's the first tournament you ever won. Don't you remember the finish?"

Max recalled his first win as a professional. "That just might work!" He leaned over to hug his father. Then he picked up his walkie-talkie.

"Scott, I need your help. Get as many people together as you can."

* * *

Josh was tied in his match against his father when they came to the seventeenth tee. Josh knew that his dad had been lucky on the twelfth hole when he won the hole by pitching in out of the hazard, but there was no excuse for letting him win two more holes to square the match. It was time to put the hammer down.

The seventeenth hole was a long par three, down in a valley running alongside the river. With the failing light, it was getting more difficult to see the green.

Bruce played first and hit his shot on the green about ten feet from the hole. The old man was not going to go down without a fight. The pressure was all on Josh now. He mumbled something to himself as he took his practice swings. Then he hit a high draw that landed on the green and rolled up toward the hole, about eight feet away.

"Nice shot," Bruce said.

Bruce hit a good putt, but it slid by the hole on the high side. In the dim light, it was getting harder and harder to read the greens.

Josh only took a few seconds to line up his shot. Once again, he mumbled something to himself when he stroked his putt. The ball rolled into the centre of the cup. Josh was now one up.

On eighteen, Josh crushed his drive. He knew his father would never be able to match that drive.

Bruce took an aggressive line and hit a good tee shot, but he didn't have the distance to clear the bunker. The ball buried in the trap, close to the lip. All he could do was pitch the ball back into the fairway.

When his father missed the green on his third shot, Josh knew he had him. *Keep your focus.* He pulled his wedge and took dead aim at the pin, then hit a beautiful shot that rolled up to within a few feet from the hole. He saw his father's shoulders slump.

He'd been trying his whole life to beat his father, but now that he was on the cusp of achieving his goal, he felt a little sad. This was the man that had first shown him how to grip the club properly when he was ten years old, taken him to God knows how many par-3 pitch-n-putt courses until he was good enough to play on the bigger courses, and spent countless hours helping him search through the rough for his errant golf balls when he was learning to hit the driver.

His hero was about to fall. The torch was being passed from father to son, the natural evolution. The problem was, Josh wasn't sure he wanted it just yet.

He remembered watching the 2009 British Open on TV with his father. That was the year 59-year-old Tom Watson, who had already won the Open five times in his career, was faced with an eight-foot putt on the last hole to win it again. It didn't seem to matter that his last major championship victory had come twenty-six years earlier. Golf is one of the few sports where an old guy can legitimately compete against much younger competitors, provided he can find the magic once again. Josh knew his father wanted Watson to make that putt. Even Josh wanted him to him to make it. Hell, the *whole world* wanted to see him roll it in. But it wasn't to be.

Josh watched his father look at his lie in the rough. He had only missed the green by a few yards, but it was a pretty ugly lie. He needed to chip it in the hole to have any chance of winning. Josh had seen him do it many times before to beat him. He found himself hoping he would do it again. A victory lap. He deserved it.

Bruce took a few practice swings with his lob wedge, the face laid wide open. He took an aggressive swing, but the ball barely moved a foot.

Bruce smiled, removed his cap, and extended his hand. "Congratulations, son. You played a great match. I'm so proud of you."

The match was over. Bruce had conceded.

Josh felt numb as he shook his father's hand. Now he knew how Stewart Cink must have felt when he won the 2009 Open Championship, the one that everyone, possibly including Cink himself, was hoping Tom Watson would win.

To the fans watching from around the green, it must have looked confusing. Bruce was beaming with pride at his son's accomplishment. Josh looked completely drained of energy and in shock.

"What was that you kept mumbling to yourself?" Bruce asked his son as they walked off the green.

"Ernie Els", Josh said. "It's just something to help me keep my tempo. The pro suggested it when he gave me the putting lesson. I'd forgotten all about it until you gave me the golf bag. Whenever I had a pressure shot, I'd just say *Ern-ie Els* to myself to keep the tempo. Someone once told me golf is all about tempo and timing."

"Sounds like someone gave you some good advice."

"You sure did, Dad."

* * *

Cheech was approaching the sixteenth green in his match against Stryker. They had both heard the cheers of the crowd on the holes ahead of them, but they had no idea what that meant. Had the Challenge Cup already been decided?

Cheech knew he had to block those thoughts from his mind and concentrate on his own match. He was two down to Stryker, with three holes to play. Not an enviable situation to be in.

Cheech thought back to what Maggie had said. "It ain't over 'til it's over."

Both Cheech and Stryker were facing birdie putts of about fifteen feet. Stryker went first, but his putt came up short. *It wasn't like him to leave a birdie putt short. Maybe he was feeling the pressure as well.*

When Cheech hit his putt, he felt like he pushed it a bit, but it broke a little more than he expected and curled into the hole. In this case, two wrongs had resulted in a right. He was now only one down to Stryker.

As they were walking off the green, Max came racing over in his golf cart.

"How are you doing?" Max said.

"I got lucky there," Cheech said, "so I'm only one down."

"Well, it's all up to you now. Ray won his match, but Bruce lost to his son, so we're all tied up in points."

Cheech looked back up the hill to the darkening sky. "I'm not sure it will matter anyway. It's getting too dark to see anything."

"Don't worry about that," Max said. "We've got that covered." He patted his father on the shoulder. "Thanks to Dad."

Cheech and Stryker walked down the darkened pathway toward the seventeenth tee. When they got there, they were surprised to see several cars surrounding the green with their headlights on. The green was lit up like it was high noon.

"I've never seen anything like this in my life," Stryker said, "but I think it might work."

Both players hit good tee shots onto the green. However, putting was more of a challenge than they thought it would be. When Stryker bent down to line up his putt, he found himself staring directly into the headlights of one of the cars. It threw him off and he missed his putt by a good foot.

Cheech was a little more fortunate. Because this was his home course, he knew his putt was straight uphill. He put a good stroke on it and the putt rolled into the hole.

Match all square, one hole to play.

"It's one thing to light up a green on a par three," Stryker said as they climbed the hill to the eighteenth tee, "but I'm not sure how they're going to light up an entire par four."

When they crested the hill, there must have been thirty cars lining both sides of the fairway. Scott had asked everyone still in the clubhouse to get into their vehicles and drive out to light up the way home. He'd even called a few of the condo owners to help out. The fairway and green were now lit up like a football stadium.

Unfortunately, the tee was almost in complete darkness. Cheech put his tee in the ground and prepared to hit.

"I'm sorry," he said, "but I can barely see my ball. Is there any way to get some light on the tee?"

Max had been worried about lighting up the fairway and the green so they could see where the ball landed. He hadn't positioned any cars around the tee.

"I got this," Maggie said.

She went running back down the hill toward the seventeenth hole. A few seconds later they heard the roar of the little red sports car as it came racing back up the hill. Everyone groaned when they heard the grinding sound when she tried to shift into second gear. And everyone jumped out of the way when she crested the hill and came flying over the back of the tee. She jammed on the brakes, leaving a huge skid mark on the tee.

"Sorry about that," she said as she jumped out of the car. "Let's not tell the greens-keeper who did this, okay?"

The crowd chuckled.

"And Cheech, sorry about your transmission. Shifting into second always seems to give me trouble."

"Don't worry about it," Cheech said. "I'm planning to trade it in anyway."

They now had enough light on the tee so they could see the ball. Cheech hit a good tee shot and found the fairway.

Stryker seemed a little flustered. He was a firm believer of having a set routine before hitting a golf shot and being in complete control of the situation. But the situation was now almost complete chaos and he pulled his tee shot into the left bunker. He took a few deep breaths to regain his composure and hit his second onto the green, leaving a long birdie putt.

When Cheech reached his tee shot, he found himself waffling between hitting a hard eight iron or an easy seven. He tried not to, but his thoughts drifted back to his shank on the fifteenth hole. *God, please don't let me shank this one.*

He stood over the ball, then backed away, then stepped back in. He decided his target was the light on the top of the clubhouse. *Just hit it toward the light.*

He felt like he made good contact and the ball shot off the clubface. It started off on line, but then he lost sight of it as it rose above the lights of the cars surrounding the green.

Where the hell was it? Was it ever going to come down?

Cheech never did see it land, but the roar of the crowd told him it must have landed on the green. He wondered how long a putt he would have. When they walked toward the green, Cheech finally located his ball and saw he had about a twenty footer left.

Stryker's putt was a little farther away, but it was probably an easier putt because it was straight up hill. Cheech fully expected him to make it and couldn't bear to watch. Even though the green was now completely surrounded by spectators, the place had gone eerily quiet. It even seemed like the wind that always blew on the course had decided to stop for the next few minutes to watch the outcome of the match.

Cheech heard the sound of the putter making contact. He heard the murmuring of the crowd grow as the ball got closer to the hole and then their groans when it slid by the edge.

Cheech now had a putt to win the match. He heard Bruce yell from the crowd, "Come on Cheech, you can make it!"

Cheech's ball was about twenty feet from the hole, but it was a tricky putt to read. It looked like it should break about a foot and a half to the right in the first part of the putt, but then straighten out when it got closer to the hole. He walked around the green several times, surveying the line from every angle. Although the car headlights lit up the green, they also seemed to distort everything. He was getting a different read each time he looked at it.

He closed his eyes trying to visualize the putt. *See it, feel it, trust it.* When he opened his eyes again, it was like the line of the putt had been magically drawn in bright lights on the green, like a pilot suddenly seeing the runway lights as he emerged from the clouds during a landing.

Cheech took a deep breath and stepped up to the ball. He made a good stroke and saw the ball follow the imaginary line he had in his head. *Had he hit it hard enough?* When it took the break and rolled back down toward the hole, he suddenly thought he might have hit it *too* hard. It was picking up more speed the closer it got to the hole. *Oh, No. He had hit it too hard!* When it hit the back of the hole, the ball popped up in the air, seemingly defying the laws of gravity for a split second before it fell back down into the hole.

Cheech just stood there, speechless. He didn't hear the roar of the crowd around the green. He didn't see Max throw his arms in the air as if he had just scored the winning touchdown in the Super Bowl. His eyes were still glazed over when Stryker removed his cap and shook his hand.

Suddenly he was sent flying as Maggie tackled him. "You did it, you did it!" she shouted as she landed on top of him. "See, I told you it wasn't over 'til it's over."

CHAPTER 27: THE BACK NINE

A few days later, Jerry was standing at his starter's podium looking at the tee sheet. It was a perfect autumn day which meant the tee sheet was almost completely filled. He was scrambling to find a spot for a walk-on. He saw Cheech, Bruce and Ray on the putting green and headed over to talk to them.

"I've got a new member looking for a game," Jerry said. "He just bought one of the condos over by the eleventh hole. Is it okay if I put him in your group?"

The three of them looked over Jerry's shoulder at the guy standing near the clubhouse. He had his back to them, so they couldn't get a clear look at him until he turned around.

"Stryker!" they all said in unison.

Stryker smiled. "Yeah, I'm back. I heard your club had a bunch of old farts playing here and was looking to add some fresh, young talent."

"Young?" Bruce questioned. "If you just bought a condo in here, it means you're at least fifty."

"Not until next month," Stryker said, "but they said

they'd waive the restriction for the time being."

"What about your membership at Blackhawk Ridge?" Ray asked. "Did your new firm finally realize what a pain in the ass you are and can you?"

Stryker didn't seemed fazed at all by the insult. "No, I seem to be fitting in quite nicely at HMT and I still use the corporate membership to take clients out for a round at Blackhawk Ridge, but I missed golfing with my friends back here."

"Friends," Bruce said. "You have friends?"

Stryker had missed the constant chirping. They all started walking toward the first tee.

"Welcome to the club," Cheech said. "Let me tell you what you're in for."

"I've played here before," Stryker said. "I know all about the course."

"Not the golf course, stupid, the over-fifty club. We'll help you with everything you need to know. First off, when's the last time you had those eyebrows trimmed? They're starting to look a little bushy."

"I'll introduce you to my physiotherapist," Bruce added. "It's just matter of time until you've got him on speed-dial."

"When's the last time you had your prostate checked?" Ray asked with a grin.

Stryker stopped. "This may have been a mistake."

* * *

After they'd finished their round, all four of them headed toward the parking lot.

"New car?" Bruce asked Cheech.

"Yeah, I traded the sports car in for this RAV4. I love it. It's much more practical and I can fit more than one set of clubs in the back."

"My brother has one," Ray said. "He loves his, too. You guys up for another round tomorrow at ten?"

Bruce and Stryker both nodded their agreement.

"I can't," Cheech said. "I'm moving."

"Moving where?" Bruce asked.

Cheech felt his face flush a little. "Back in with Maggie. We're going to give it another shot."

"Good for you," Bruce said.

* * *

The next day, Bruce was standing on the first tee with Ray and Stryker when he heard the trunk of a car slam shut. Bruce smiled when he saw who it was.

"I hope you guys don't mind, but I asked my son Josh to join us today. I knew we'd have a spot open with Cheech moving today."

"No problem," Ray said.

Josh came racing over to the tee. "Sorry I'm late." He tipped his cap to Ray and Stryker. "So what's the game today?"

"How about you and Stryker take on me and Ray?" Bruce said.

"Sounds good," Josh said.

"But you guys have to give us two shots each," Bruce added.

"What?" Josh asked. "Why should we give you two shots?"

"Because you're both younger than we are. You can't expect us old fogies to beat you guys straight up. I think two shots sounds about right."

"I think we're getting sandbagged," Stryker said. "How about one shot each?"

Bruce and Ray nodded to each other.

"Done," Bruce said as he pulled out his driver. He

grinned at Josh. "It'll be like taking candy from a baby."

Josh grinned back. "Bring it on, old man."

* * *

Later that afternoon, Jerry ambled back into the pro shop. After a busy morning, things had finally started to slow down. Most of the remaining bookings were for husbands and wives looking to head out for a quick nine together before supper.

Jerry was hoping to sneak in nine holes himself. People who worked at the club were allowed to play for free once a week, but only after three in the afternoon. Jerry could have asked to play with one of the couples about to tee off, but he didn't want to impose.

"Any chance I could sneak out on the back nine?" Jerry asked Scott.

Scott looked at the bookings to see who was about to make the turn at the ninth hole.

"The group that just finished the ninth hole aren't playing eighteen," Scott said, "and I think the ladies coming up to the green are only going to play nine as well. You should be good to go."

Jerry headed to his car to grab his clubs. He purchased a sandwich at the snack bar and headed to the tenth tee. Sandwiches had become his standard supper of late. It didn't seem worth it to cook a meal just for himself.

He had just teed off on the tenth hole when a golf cart pulled up. It was Anne-Marie Tremblay.

"Sorry," Jerry said. "I didn't mean to cut in. I thought your group was only going to play nine. You can go ahead and play through."

"No problem," Anne-Marie said. "The rest of my group quit after nine, but I wanted to keep going. I've got a good score going."

Anne-Marie hit her tee shot.

"Why don't we play together?" she asked. "There's some really treacherous holes on the back nine. No one should have to face them alone."

Jerry nodded his agreement. Truer words were never spoken.

OTHER BOOKS BY

E.A. BRIGINSHAW

Goliath

Henry Shaw leads a relatively quiet life trying to balance his work at a growing law firm with his family life, including supporting his teenage son who has a promising soccer career ahead of him. But all of that changes when Henry's bipolar brother, in one of his manic states, tells him that Goliath didn't really die as told in the biblical story – and that he is Goliath.

When his brother disappears along with a media magnate, the FBI and the local police believe they may have been part of a secret international network and that Goliath was his brother's code name. The solution to this puzzle may reside in his brother's laptop computer, which mysteriously disappears during a break-in at his house.

Is his brother dead or just hiding from forces trying to destroy the network? Henry tries to solve the puzzle along with an intriguing woman he encounters at an airport bar.

Goliath is available for purchase on the Amazon.com website.
Book   (ISBN 978-0-9921390-0-1)
eBook (ISBN 978-0-9921390-1-8)

The Second Shooter

It has been widely speculated that the FBI, CIA and Secret Service have been hiding the existence of critical evidence as to those involved in the assassination of President John F. Kennedy. The JFK Records Act requires that all records related to the assassination be released to the public by October 26, 2017, unless the President deems their release would cause grave harm to the nation. When some of these potentially dangerous records are accidentally released, forces within the government attempt to recover them using whatever means necessary, including the elimination of anyone who may have seen them.

In the sequel to "Goliath", David and Robert Shaw head off to university and find themselves drawn into the world of shadow governments and secret societies. Despite the work of an investigative journalist to uncover the truth, and the efforts of their father to protect them, they find themselves squarely in the crosshairs of "The Second Shooter".

The Second Shooter is available for purchase on the Amazon.com website.
Book   (ISBN 978-0-9921390-4-9)
eBook (ISBN 978-0-9921390-5-6)

The Legacy

Life is pretty good for the Baxter boys. Eric Baxter is a recent college graduate starting his career in financial planning. His younger brother, Chip, is a promising athlete heading off to compete at the Olympic Games in Brazil. And their father, Brian, has accumulated a tidy sum of money over his life.

As Eric prepares to start managing his father's money, he learns that his father's most important objective is to leave a legacy. But when Eric and his brother are kidnapped along with several other people while on a tour in Brazil, the legacy is in jeopardy.

Will the hostages be rescued before the final deadline is reached? Will Brian go against the recommendations of the FBI and the Brazilian police and pay the ransom? Their fate is determined in "The Legacy".

The Legacy is available for purchase on the Amazon.com website.
Book (ISBN 978-0-9921390-2-5)
eBook (ISBN 978-0-9921390-3-2)